Build & Extend Your Korean Sentences

점점 길어지는 한국어 문장

Written by
Talk To Me In Korean

Build & Extend Your Korean Sentences
점점 길어지는 한국어 문장

1판 1쇄 · 1st edition published	2021. 1. 11.	
1판 6쇄 · 6th edition published	2024. 6. 24.	
지은이 · Written by	Talk To Me In Korean	
책임편집 · Edited by	선경화 Kyung-hwa Sun, 석다혜 Dahye Seok, 김은희 Eunhee Kim	
디자인 · Designed by	선윤아 Yoona Sun	
삽화 · Illustrations by	배지혜 Jihye Bae	
녹음 · Voice Recordings by	석다혜 Dahye Seok, 문준배 Joonbae Moon	
펴낸곳 · Published by	롱테일북스 Longtail Books	
펴낸이 · Publisher	이수영 Su Young Lee	
편집 · Copy-edited by	김보경 Florence Kim	
주소 · Addres	04033 서울특별시 마포구 양화로 113, 3층(서교동, 순흥빌딩)	
	3rd Floor, 113 Yanghwa-ro, Mapo-gu, Seoul, KOREA	
이메일 · E-mail	TTMIK@longtailbooks.co.kr	
ISBN	979-11-86701-92-8 13710	

*이 교재의 내용을 사전 허가 없이 전재하거나 복제할 경우 법적인 제재를 받게 됨을 알려 드립니다.

*잘못된 책은 구입하신 서점이나 본사에서 교환해 드립니다.

*정가는 표지에 표시되어 있습니다.

TTMIK - TALK TO ME IN KOREAN

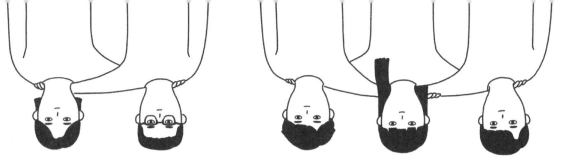

Build & Extend Your Korean Sentences

by adding, modifying, combining, and changing!

Written by
Talk To Me In Korean

점점 길 — 어지는 한국어 문장

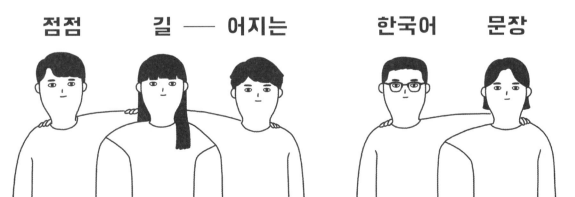

/ Table of Contents

01. 조금 추워서 따뜻한 이불을 덮었는데, 더워서 땀이 났어요.

Since it was a little cold, I covered (myself) with a warm blanket, but then I was hot, so I sweated.

02. 급하게 면도하다가 작은 상처가 나서 약을 발라야 돼요.

I got a small cut while I was shaving in a hurry, so I have to apply medicine.

03. 수염이 짧아도 매일 면도해야 돼서 아침에 항상 바빠요.

Even if my stubble is short, I have to shave every day, so I am always busy in the morning.

04. 다래끼가 더 커지기 전에 집 앞에 있는 안과에 가서 치료를 받으세요.

Before your stye gets bigger, go to the ophthalmologist in front of your house and get treatment.

05. 학교에 늦지 않으려고 서서 양말을 신다가 넘어졌어요.

I fell over while I was putting on my socks standing up in order not to be late for school.

06. 물놀이하면 화장이 전부 지워질 것 같으니까 화장품을 챙겨야겠어요.

Since I think my makeup will come off completely if I play in the water, I think I should pack my cosmetics.

07. 아침에 일어나자마자 가볍게 운동하고 시원한 커피를 마신 다음에 회사에 가요.

As soon as I get up in the morning, I exercise lightly and drink cold coffee, and then I go to work.

/ Preface

Learning a new language is a fantastic journey, but it can take a long time. So if you want to learn to speak Korean in an efficient and effective way, you need to know what to practice first. You will eventually need to learn about various aspects of the Korean language, but if you really want to start speaking Korean in real-life situations as soon as possible, this book will give you exactly what you need.

This book focuses on helping you develop your Korean through practicing making increasingly longer sentences, so that you can convey your thoughts and ideas in more complete and complex ways. In addition, all the words used in the practice sentences are related to everyday activities and actions that you do on a regular basis. So with this book, you can achieve two goals at the same time — practice making Korean sentences more flexibly, while also learning essential vocabulary and expressions for activities in your daily life.

As you study with this book, make sure you practice saying everything out loud. And since the sentences in the book are all very practical and realistic, imagine yourself saying them to someone you know. This way, when you actually find yourself in a similar real-life situation, you will be able to say everything more confidently.

Thank you for choosing Talk To Me In Korean and we hope you enjoy learning with our book!

/ How to Use This Book

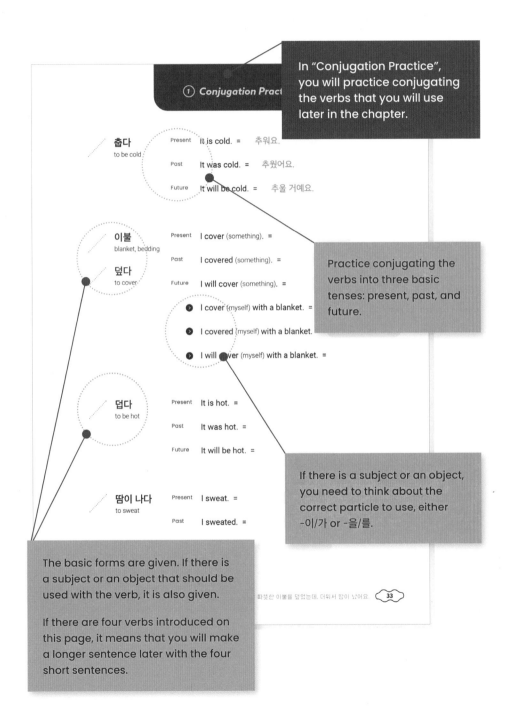

In "Conjugation Practice", you will practice conjugating the verbs that you will use later in the chapter.

① *Conjugation Prac...*

춥다
to be cold

Present	It is cold. =	추워요.
Past	It was cold. =	추웠어요.
Future	It will be cold. =	추울 거예요.

이불
blanket, bedding

덮다
to cover

Present	I cover (something). =
Past	I covered (something). =
Future	I will cover (something). =

Practice conjugating the verbs into three basic tenses: present, past, and future.

❯ I cover (myself) with a blanket. =
❯ I covered (myself) with a blanket. =
❯ I will cover (myself) with a blanket. =

덥다
to be hot

Present	It is hot. =
Past	It was hot. =
Future	It will be hot. =

If there is a subject or an object, you need to think about the correct particle to use, either -이/가 or -을/를.

땀이 나다
to sweat

Present	I sweat. =
Past	I sweated. =

The basic forms are given. If there is a subject or an object that should be used with the verb, it is also given.

If there are four verbs introduced on this page, it means that you will make a longer sentence later with the four short sentences.

따뜻한 이불을 덮었는데, 더워서 땀이 났어요. ⟨33⟩

You can check out the answers on the following page.

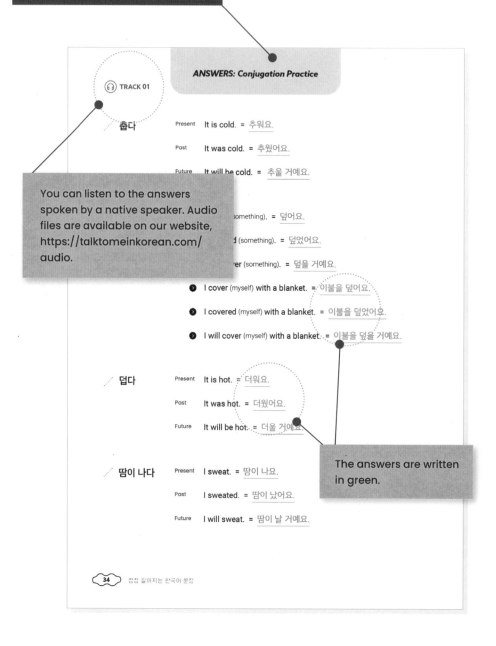

ANSWERS: Conjugation Practice

TRACK 01

춥다

Present	It is cold. = 추워요.
Past	It was cold. = 추웠어요.
Future	It will be cold. = 추울 거예요.

You can listen to the answers spoken by a native speaker. Audio files are available on our website, https://talktomeinkorean.com/audio.

... something). = 덮어요.
... d (something). = 덮었어요.
... ver (something). = 덮을 거예요.

● I cover (myself) with a blanket. = 이불을 덮어요.
● I covered (myself) with a blanket. = 이불을 덮었어요.
● I will cover (myself) with a blanket. = 이불을 덮을 거예요.

덥다

Present	It is hot. = 더워요.
Past	It was hot. = 더웠어요.
Future	It will be hot. = 더울 거예요.

The answers are written in green.

땀이 나다

Present	I sweat. = 땀이 나요.
Past	I sweated. = 땀이 났어요.
Future	I will sweat. = 땀이 날 거예요.

In "Extension Practice", you'll see how sentences can become longer and longer by adding, modifying, changing, or combining!

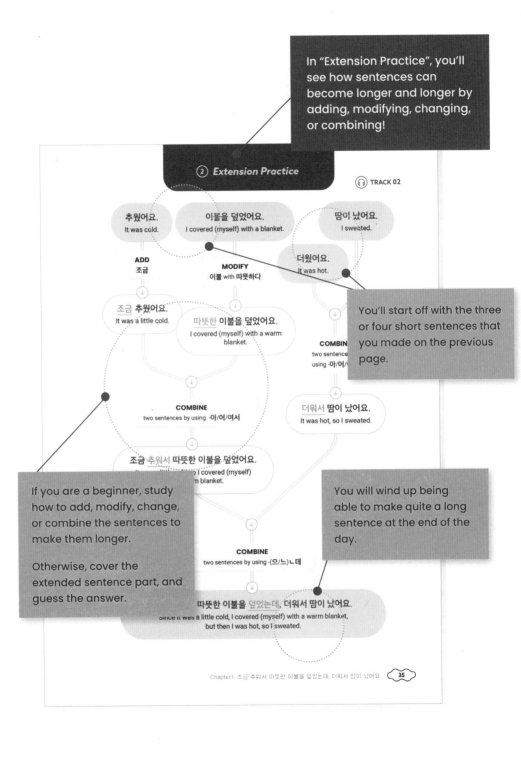

② *Extension Practice*

🎧 TRACK 02

추웠어요.
It was cold.

이불을 덮었어요.
I covered (myself) with a blanket.

땀이 났어요.
I sweated.

더웠어요.
It was hot.

ADD
조금

MODIFY
이불 with 따뜻하다

조금 추웠어요.
It was a little cold.

따뜻한 이불을 덮었어요.
I covered (myself) with a warm blanket.

You'll start off with the three or four short sentences that you made on the previous page.

COMBINE
two sentences
using -아/어/

COMBINE
two sentences by using -아/어/여서

더워서 땀이 났어요.
It was hot, so I sweated.

조금 추워서 따뜻한 이불을 덮었어요.
~~~~~~~~~~~ I covered (myself)
~ m blanket.

If you are a beginner, study how to add, modify, change, or combine the sentences to make them longer.

Otherwise, cover the extended sentence part, and guess the answer.

You will wind up being able to make quite a long sentence at the end of the day.

COMBINE
two sentences by using -(으/느)ㄴ데

따뜻한 이불을 덮었는데, 더워서 땀이 났어요.
Since it was a little cold, I covered (myself) with a warm blanket,
but then I was hot, so I sweated.

Chapter1. 조금 추워서 따뜻한 이불을 덮었는데, 더워서 땀이 났어요.　35

Review what you practiced on
the previous page here.

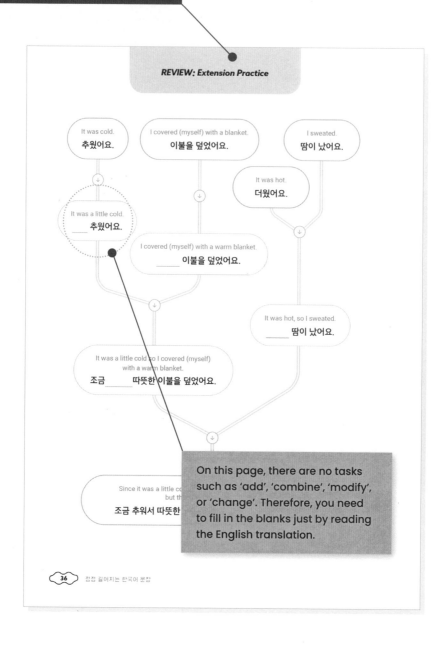

REVIEW: Extension Practice

It was cold.
추웠어요.

I covered (myself) with a blanket.
이불을 덮었어요.

I sweated.
땀이 났어요.

It was hot.
더웠어요.

It was a little cold.
____ **추웠어요.**

I covered (myself) with a warm blanket.
____ **이불을 덮었어요.**

It was hot, so I sweated.
____ **땀이 났어요.**

It was a little cold so I covered (myself)
with a warm blanket.
조금____ **따뜻한 이불을 덮었어요.**

On this page, there are no tasks
such as 'add', 'combine', 'modify',
or 'change'. Therefore, you need
to fill in the blanks just by reading
the English translation.

Since it was a little c
but th
조금 추워서 따뜻한

In "Speaking Practice", you can practice speaking by using the sentences that you made on the previous page.

③ *Speaking Practice*

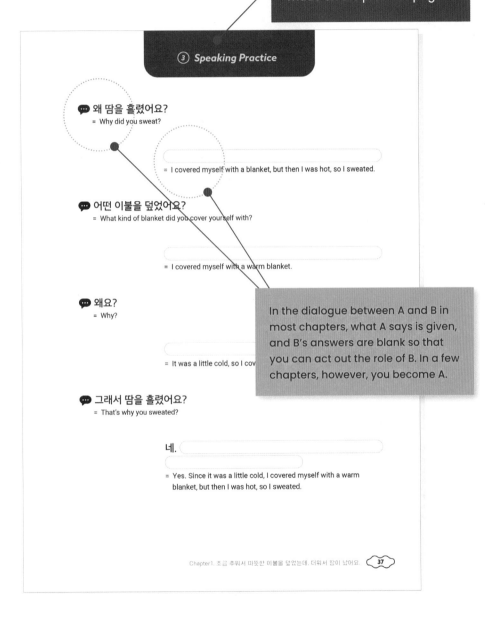

💬 왜 땀을 흘렸어요?
= Why did you sweat?

= I covered myself with a blanket, but then I was hot, so I sweated.

💬 어떤 이불을 덮었어요?
= What kind of blanket did you cover yourself with?

= I covered myself with a warm blanket.

💬 왜요?
= Why?

= It was a little cold, so I cov[...]

In the dialogue between A and B in most chapters, what A says is given, and B's answers are blank so that you can act out the role of B. In a few chapters, however, you become A.

💬 그래서 땀을 흘렸어요?
= That's why you sweated?

네.

= Yes. Since it was a little cold, I covered myself with a warm blanket, but then I was hot, so I sweated.

On this page, both check your answers, and also listen to the dialogue and repeat after the native speaker using the audio files on our website.

ANSWERS: Speaking Practice

🎧 TRACK 03

💬 왜 땀을 흘렸어요?
= Why did you sweat?

💬 이불을 덮었는데, 더워서 땀이 났어요.
= I covered myself with a blanket, but then I was hot, so I sweated.

💬 어떤 이불을 덮었어요?
= What kind of blanket did you cover yourself with?

💬 따뜻한 이불을 덮었어요.
= I covered myself with a warm blanket.

💬 왜요?
= Why?

💬 조금 추워서 따뜻한 이불을 덮었어요.
= It was a little cold, so I covered myself with a warm blanket.

💬 그래서 땀을 흘렸어요?
= That's why you sweated?

💬 네. 조금 추워서 따뜻한 이불을 덮었는데, 더워서 땀이 났어요.
= Yes. Since it was a little cold, I covered myself with a warm blanket, but then I was hot, so I sweated.

Conjugation Practice ··

1. Conjugation of Regular Verbs/Adjectives

The infinitive form (also known as the "dictionary form") of Korean verbs and adjectives always ends with -다. The "verb/adjective stem" is formed by simply dropping the -다 from the infinitive form of a verb or adjective. For most verb and adjective conjugations in Korean, you take the "verb/adjective stem" of a verb or adjective and add various endings to it.

Present Tense: -아/어/여요

To create a sentence in the present tense, add -아요, -어요, or -여요 after the verb/adjective stem. If the verb/adjective stem's last vowel is ㅏ or ㅗ, it is followed by -아요. If the stem's last vowel is NOT ㅏ or ㅗ, it is followed by -어요. Only one verb/adjective stem, 하, is followed by -여요. However, 하여요 is always shortened to 해요.

Ex) 들어오다 = to come in

들어오 + -아요 → 들어오아요 → 들어와요. (He/she/it comes in.)

    * When ㅗ and -아 are combined, it becomes ㅘ.

슬프다 = to be sad

슬프 + -어요 → 슬프어요 → 슬퍼요. (He/she/it is sad.)

    * When ㅡ and -어 are combined, ㅡ is dropped.

어리다 = to be young, to be little

어리 + -어요 → 어리어요 → 어려요. (He/she/it is young/little.)

    * When ㅣ and -어 are combined, it becomes ㅕ.

채우다 = to fill (in/up)

채우 + -어요 → 채우어요 → 채워요. (He/she/I fill [something] in/up.)

    * When ㅜ and -어 are combined, it becomes ㅝ.

사용되다 = to be used

사용되 + -어요 → 사용되어요 → 사용돼요. (It is used.)

    * When 되 and -어 are combined, it becomes 되어, and is often shortened to 돼.

Past Tense: -았/었/였어요

Add -았어요, -었어요, or -였어요 after the verb/adjective stem to form a statement in the past tense. If the last vowel of the verb/adjective stem is ㅏ or ㅗ, it is followed by -았어요. If the last vowel is NOT ㅏ or ㅗ, it is followed by -었어요. Only one verb/adjective stem, 하, is followed by -였어요, creating 하였어요. However, 하였어요 is usually shortened to 했어요.

Ex) 들어오다 = to come in

들어오 + -았어요 → 들어오았어요 → 들어왔어요. (He/she/it came in.)

슬프다 = to be sad

슬프 + -었어요 → 슬프었어요 → 슬펐어요. (He/she/it was sad.)

어리다 = to be young, to be little

어리 + -었어요 → 어리었어요 → 어렸어요. (He/she/I was young/little.)

채우다 = to fill (in/up)

채우 + -었어요 → 채우었어요 → 채웠어요. (He/she/I filled [something] in/up.)

사용되다 = to be used

사용되 + -었어요 → 사용되었어요 → 사용됐어요. (It was used.)

Future Tense: -(으)ㄹ 거예요

To create a sentence in the future tense, add either -을 거예요 or -ㄹ 거예요. If the last syllable of the verb stem is a consonant, add -을 거예요. If the verb stem ends with a vowel, add -ㄹ 거예요.

Ex) 들어오다 = to come in
들어오 + -ㄹ 거예요 → 들어올 거예요. (I will come in.)

읽다 = to read
읽 + -을 거예요 → 읽을 거예요. (I will read.)

2. Conjugation of Irregular Verbs/Adjectives

Irregulars: ㅂ

If the verb/adjective stem ends with ㅂ, and is followed by a conjugation that starts with a vowel, the ㅂ changes to 우.

Ex) 무섭다 = to be scary, to be scared
Present Tense: 무섭 + -어요 → 무서우 + -어요 → 무서우어요 → 무서워요.
Past Tense: 무섭 + -었어요 → 무서우 + -었어요 → 무서우었어요 → 무서웠어요.
Future Tense: 무섭 + -(으)ㄹ 거예요 → 무서우 + -(으)ㄹ 거예요 → 무서울 거예요.

Irregulars: 르

If the verb/adjective stem ends with 르, and is followed by a conjugation that starts with -아/어/여- or -았/었/였-, the 르 is changed to ㄹ and is placed at the end of the previous vowel. One more ㄹ is needed before adding the verb conjugation ending.

Ex) 고르다 = to choose; to pick; to select

    Present Tense: 고르 + -아요 → 골ㄹ + -아요 → 골라요.

    Past Tense: 고르 + -았어요 → 골ㄹ + -았어요 → 골랐어요.

    Future Tense: 고르 + -(으)ㄹ 거예요 → 고를 거예요.

Irregulars: ㅎ

If the adjective stem ends with ㅎ, and is followed by a conjugation that starts with a vowel, the ㅎ is dropped. If the conjugation starts with -아/어-, not only is ㅎ dropped, but -아/어- changes to -애/에-.

Ex) 노랗다 = to be yellow

    Present Tense: 노랗 + -아요 → 노라 + -애요 → 노라애요 → 노래요.

    Past Tense: 노랗 + -았어요 → 노라 + -앴어요 → 노라앴어요 → 노랬어요.

    Future Tense: 노랗 + -(으)ㄹ 거예요 → 노라 + -(으)ㄹ 거예요 → 노랄 거예요.

3. Particles

Subject Marking Particles: -이/가

Subject marking particles are placed after a noun to indicate that THAT noun is the subject of the sentence. If the noun ends with a consonant, it is followed by -이. If the noun ends with a vowel, it is followed by -가.

Ex) 하늘 = sky, 파랗다 = to be blue

    하늘이 파래요. = The sky is blue.

    가위 = scissors, 작다 = to be small

    가위가 작아요. = The scissors are small.

Object Marking Particles: -을/를

Object marking particles are placed after a noun to indicate that THAT noun is the direct object of the verb in the sentence. If the noun ends with a consonant, it is followed by -을. If the noun ends with a vowel, it is followed by -를.

Ex) 하늘 = sky, 보다 = to look
하늘을 봤어요. = I looked at the sky.

가위 = scissors, 사다 = to buy
가위를 샀어요. = I bought a pair of scissors.

Adverbial Marking Particle (1): -에

There are many adverbial marking particles in Korean, and -에 is one of the particles that has many different functions.

First, it is used to mark locations, and it is placed after a noun to indicate that THAT noun is the location where something "is" or "exists", or is the direction that one is going toward.

Ex) 학교에 있어요. = I am at school.
학교에 가요. = I go to school.

It is also placed after a noun to indicate that THAT noun is an object that causes a certain action.

Ex) 거짓말에 속았어요. = I was deceived by his/her lie.
그 의견에 찬성해요. = I agree with that opinion.

Adverbial Marking Particle (2): -(으)로

This particle is used to mark the means or tools by which something is done. -으로 is placed after a noun that ends with a consonant, and -로 is placed after a noun that ends with a vowel.

Ex) 가위로 머리를 잘랐어요. = I cut my hair with scissors.
　　핸드폰으로 사진을 찍었어요. = I took a photo with my mobile phone.

Extension Practice ···

1. ADD

You can extend your sentence by adding an adverbial, which is a word or a group of words that modifies or more closely defines the sentence or the verb.

You could just add an adverb.

Ex) 너무 밝아요. = It is too bright.

Or you could make an adverbial by attaching a particle to a noun.

Ex) 5시에 일어났어요. = I got up at 5 o'clock.
　　화분에 물을 줬어요. = I watered the plants.
　　집에서 일할 거예요. = I am going to work from home.

Sometimes, you can change an adjective into an adverb by attaching -게 to an adjective stem.

Ex) 아침은 가볍게 먹어요. = I have a light breakfast.
　　급하게 어디 가요? = Where are you going in a rush?

2. MODIFY

You can also extend your sentence by adding an adnominal, which is a word or phrase that qualifies a noun, such as an adjective or a relative clause.

If you use a determiner, you do not have to conjugate it.

Ex) 새 = new (determiner)
　　 새 신발 = new shoes

　　 한 = one (determiner)
　　 한 사람 = one person

However, if you use an adjective, you need to conjugate it from its infinitive/dictionary form first. This is because the basic form of Korean adjectives found in the dictionary is actually a descriptive verb form that means, "to be + adjective". In order to change the descriptive verb into an adjective, you can simply drop the -다 and add either -ㄴ or -은. If the verb stem ends with a vowel, you add -ㄴ. If the verb stem ends with a consonant, you add -은.

Ex) 크다 = to be big (adjective in the infinitive form)
　　 큰 = big (base adjective form)
　　 큰 집 = big house

　　 높다 = to be high (adjective in the infinitive form)
　　 높은 = high (base adjective form)
　　 높은 산 = high mountain

The descriptive verbs 있다 and 없다, including verbs that end in -있다 and -없다, are an exception because they are conjugated with -는.

Ex) 없다 = to not exist, to not have (adjective in the infinitive form)
　　 없는 = does not exist; does not have (base adjective form)
　　 창문 없는 집 = a house that does not have windows

맛있다 = to be tasty (adjective in the infinitive form)

맛있는 = tasty (base adjective form)

맛있는 점심 = tasty lunch

Adnominal Marking Particle: -의

-의 is a particle that shows possession, belonging, origin, or characteristics, and basically means "of". The word order for -의 or "of", however, is very different in Korean and English. If you say "A of B", in Korean you need to switch it to "B의 A". To make it simpler, you can just think of -의 as the possessive 's, as in "my friend's house", "my teacher's name", etc.

Ex) 학기의 시작 = the beginning of a semester

저의 작품 = my work (저의 is often shortened to 제)

3. COMBINE

You can also extend your sentences by combining two sentences through the use of connective endings. Following are the connective endings used in this book.

-아/어/여서

(1) Reason + -아/어/여서 + result

Please note that -아/어/여서 can only be attached to a verb stem. When connecting two sentences using -아/어/여서, the first sentence cannot include other endings like -았/었/였- or -겠-.

Ex) 비가 왔어요. (It rained.) + -아/어/여서 + 못 갔어요. (I couldn't go.)

= 비가 와서 못 갔어요. (O) It rained, so I couldn't go.

* 비가 왔어서 못 갔어요. (X)

(2) An action + -아/어/여서 + another action that takes place after the first action

Please note that the two actions are not independent of each other. Rather, the first action causes the second action to happen.

Ex) 공원에 갈 거예요. (I'm going to the park.) + 책을 읽을 거예요. (I'm going to read a book.)

= 공원에 가서 책을 읽을 거예요. I will go to the park and read a book.

-고

You can use -고 to link two statements about events when one of the events follows the other. Please note that it is unnatural to use the same tense for every verb, especially when using the future tense or the past tense. Instead, it sounds more natural to use the past or future tense with just the final verb.

Ex) 씻었어요. (I washed.) + -고 + 잤어요. (I slept.)

= 씻고 잤어요. I washed and slept. (more natural)

* 씻었고 잤어요. (less natural)

-(으/느)ㄴ데

You can use -(으/느)ㄴ데 to introduce background information or to contextualize a situation before explaining something that happened. -는데 is used after action verbs, 있다, 없다, -았/었/였-, and -겠. -은데 is used after descriptive verbs which have a final consonant in the verb stem, except for the consonant ㄹ. When a descriptive verb ends in the consonant ㄹ, ㄹ is dropped and -ㄴ데 is used. -ㄴ데 is also used after descriptive verbs that end in a vowel, 이다, and 아니다.

Ex) 어제 자고 있었어요. (I was sleeping yesterday.) + -(으/느)ㄴ데 + 한국에서 전화가 왔어요. (I got a phone call from Korea.)

= 어제 자고 있었는데 한국에서 전화가 왔어요. I was sleeping yesterday, and then I got a phone call from Korea.

-기 전에

You can use -기 전에 in sentences to express "before -ing" in Korean. As with many Korean expressions and prepositions, the order is the opposite of English. In English, the word "before" comes before the clause or word, but in Korean, it comes after. Please note that -기 전에 cannot be combined with another ending such as -았/었/였- or -겠-. You can only combine -기 전에 with a verb stem.

Ex) 영화를 봤어요. (I watched a movie.) + -기 전에 + 화장실에 갔다 왔어요. (I went to the restroom.)
= 영화를 보기 전에 화장실에 갔다 왔어요. (O) I went to the restroom before watching a movie.
* 영화를 봤기 전에 화장실에 갔다 왔어요. (X)

-(으)ㄴ 다음에

You can use -(으)ㄴ 다음에 in sentences to express "after -ing" in Korean. In English, the word "after" comes before the clause or word, but in Korean, it comes after. Here, -(으)ㄴ indicates that the verb was done in the past. -은 다음에 is used after verbs that have a final consonant in the verb stem, except for the consonant ㄹ. Verbs that end in a vowel or in the consonant ㄹ are conjugated with -ㄴ 다음에 instead. In the case of the consonant ㄹ, ㄹ is also dropped before adding -ㄴ 다음에 to the verb stem.

Ex) 점심을 먹었어요. (I had lunch.) + -(으)ㄴ 다음에 + 도서관에 갔어요. (I went to the library.)
= 점심을 먹은 다음에 도서관에 갔어요. (O) After having lunch, I went to the library.
* 점심을 먹었은 다음에 도서관에 갔어요. (X)

-더니

You can use -더니 when one thing is either a sign of something else (usually bigger, more intense, or more serious), or the direct result of another thing.

점점 길어지는 한국어 문장

Ex) 책을 많이 읽었어요. (I read a lot.) + -더니 + 눈이 피곤해요. (My eyes are tired.)
= 책을 많이 읽었더니 눈이 피곤해요. I read a lot, so my eyes are tired.

-(으)니까

The verb preceding -(으)니까 is the reason or the basis of judgement for the verb after -(으)니까.

Ex) 시험 공부 열심히 했어요. (I studied hard for the exam.) + -(으)니까 + 시험 잘 볼 거예요. (I am going to do well on the exam.)
= 시험 공부 열심히 했으니까 시험 잘 볼 거예요. I studied hard for the exam, so I am going to do well on the exam.

-지만

You can use -지만 when contrasting two clauses.

Ex) 슬펐어요. (I was sad.) + -지만 + 울지 않았어요. (I didn't cry.)
= 슬펐지만 울지 않았어요. I was sad, but I didn't cry.

-(으)려면

-(으)려면 is short for -(으)려고 하면. Therefore, it means "if one is intending to..." or "if you want to be able to..."

Ex) 일찍 일어나요. (You get up early.) + -(으)려면 + 일찍 자야 돼요. (You have to go to bed early.)
= 일찍 일어나려면 일찍 자야 돼요. If you want to get up early, you have to go to bed early.

-(으)면

In order to express the meaning "if" in Korean, you need to combine a verb with -(으)면. Conditionality is expressed through the verb ending, rather than through the usage of the word "if" at the beginning of a sentence as in English.

Ex) 내일 비가 와요. (It rains tomorrow.) + -(으)면 + 집에 있을 거예요. (I will stay home.)
= 내일 비가 오면 집에 있을 거예요. If it rains tomorrow, I will stay home.

-다가

When you want to express a string of consecutive events, or things that happen simultaneously or shortly after one another, you can use the verb ending -다가. When the first action is the cause, and the second action is the effect, the effect is usually negative.

Ex) 수업 시간에 떠들었어요. (I talked during class.) + -다가 + 선생님한테 혼났어요. (I got scolded by the teacher.)
= 수업 시간에 떠들다가 선생님한테 혼났어요. I talked during class, so I got scolded by the teacher.

-아/어/여도

You can connect two sentences using -아/어/여도 when the second sentence happens regardless of the first sentence.

Ex) 바빠요. (I am busy.) + -아/어/여도 + 한국에 갈 거예요. (I will go to Korea.)
= 바빠도 한국에 갈 거예요. I will go to Korea even though I am busy.

-(으)려고

By attaching -(으)려고 to a verb stem, you can express your intention or purpose for doing something. Please note that -(으)려고 cannot be combined with another ending such as -았/었/였- or -겠-. You can only combine -(으)려고 with a verb stem.

Ex) 화장실에 갈 거예요. (I will go to the restroom.) + -(으)려고 + 일어났어요. (I stood up.)
= 화장실에 가려고 일어났어요. I stood up to go to the restroom.

-자마자

-자마자 means "as soon as (you do something)" or "right after (doing something)", and you can use it to connect a sequence of events or behaviors. Please note that -자마자 cannot be combined with another ending such as -았/었/였- or -겠-. You can only combine a verb stem with -자마자.

Ex) 집에 갔어요. (I went home.) + -자마자 + 잠들었어요. (I fell asleep.)
= 집에 가자마자 잠들었어요. I fell asleep as soon as I went home.

4. CHANGE

Unlike the three tasks above, when you change a sentence into another form, like a question or a negative sentence, you must actually change your original base sentence. In most cases in this book, you change a sentence into another form by changing the ending of the sentence. However, there are three exceptions to this rule.

A. Changing a sentence into a negative form

There are three ways to change a sentence into a negative form:

(1) adding 안 before a verb

Ex) 제가 마셨어요. = I drank.
    제가 안 마셨어요. = I didn't drink.

(2) adding -지 않다 after a verb stem

Ex) 제가 했어요. = I did it.
    제가 하지 않았어요. = I didn't do it.

(3) replacing a verb with its antonym

Ex) 시간 있어요. = I have time.
    시간 없어요. = I don't have time.

B. Changing a sentence into a question

You can simply change the period to a question mark.

Ex) 이거 지민 씨 가방이에요. = This is Jimin's bag.
    이거 지민 씨 가방이에요? = Is this Jimin's bag?

C. Changing a marker

In the "Conjugation Practice" section, you learned how to use subject marking particles and object marking particles. To change the meaning or nuance of a sentence, you can replace these subject and object marking particles with the topic marking particle -은/는.

Ex) 가위가 작아요. = The scissors are small.
        * If you change this to 가위는 작아요, you are implying that even though the scissors are small, something else is not small.

가위를 샀어요. = I bought a pair of scissors.

> * If you change this to 가위는 샀어요, you are implying that although you bought the scissors, there is something else that you did not buy.

Other than these three cases, you are asked to change a sentence ending to convey your meaning.

Ex) -(으)ㄹ래요 = want to

-(으)세요: This ending changes the sentence into a polite imperative sentence.

-아/어/여야 되다 = to have to (colloquial)

-아/어/여야 하다 = to have to (literary)

-아/어/여지다 = to become

-(으)려고 하다 = to be going to, to be planning to

-는 것 같다 = I think one does...

-(으)ㄹ 것 같다 = I think one will...

-(으)ㄴ 것 같다 = I think one did...

-아/어/여야겠다 = I think I better...

-아/어/여 보다 = to try doing something

Scan the QR code here and **listen to native speaker's pronunciation.**

If you cannot use the QR code,
you can also listen to the audio
and download it from our website,
https://talktomeinkorean.com/audio.

1

조금 추워서 따뜻한 이불을 덮었는데,
더워서 땀이 났어요.

춥다
to be cold

Present	It is cold. = 추워요.
Past	It was cold. = 추웠어요.
Future	It will be cold. = 추울 거예요.

이불
blanket, bedding

덮다
to cover

Present	I cover (something). =
Past	I covered (something). =
Future	I will cover (something). =

❯ I cover (myself) with a blanket. =

❯ I covered (myself) with a blanket. =

❯ I will cover (myself) with a blanket. =

덥다
to be hot

Present	It is hot. =
Past	It was hot. =
Future	It will be hot. =

땀이 나다
to sweat

Present	I sweat. =
Past	I sweated. =
Future	I will sweat. =

ANSWERS: Conjugation Practice

춥다

Present   It is cold. = 추워요.

Past   It was cold. = 추웠어요.

Future   It will be cold. = 추울 거예요.

이불

Present   I cover (something). = 덮어요.

Past   I covered (something). = 덮었어요.

덮다

Future   I will cover (something). = 덮을 거예요.

❯ I cover (myself) with a blanket. = 이불을 덮어요.

❯ I covered (myself) with a blanket. = 이불을 덮었어요.

❯ I will cover (myself) with a blanket. = 이불을 덮을 거예요.

덥다

Present   It is hot. = 더워요.

Past   It was hot. = 더웠어요.

Future   It will be hot. = 더울 거예요.

땀이 나다

Present   I sweat. = 땀이 나요.

Past   I sweated. = 땀이 났어요.

Future   I will sweat. = 땀이 날 거예요.

추웠어요.
It was cold.

이불을 덮었어요.
I covered (myself) with a blanket.

땀이 났어요.
I sweated.

ADD
조금

MODIFY
이불 with 따뜻하다

더웠어요.
It was hot.

↓

조금 추웠어요.
It was a little cold.

↓

따뜻한 이불을 덮었어요.
I covered (myself) with a warm blanket.

↓

COMBINE
two sentences by
using -아/어/여서

↓

COMBINE
two sentences by using -아/어/여서

더워서 땀이 났어요.
It was hot, so I sweated.

↓

조금 추워서 따뜻한 이불을 덮었어요.
It was a little cold so I covered (myself)
with a warm blanket.

↓

COMBINE
two sentences by using -(으/느)ㄴ데

↓

조금 추워서 따뜻한 이불을 덮었는데, 더워서 땀이 났어요.
Since it was a little cold, I covered (myself) with a warm blanket,
but then I was hot, so I sweated.

It was cold.
추웠어요.

I covered (myself) with a blanket.
이불을 덮었어요.

I sweated.
땀이 났어요.

It was hot.
더웠어요.

It was a little cold.
____ 추웠어요.

I covered (myself) with a warm blanket.
_____ 이불을 덮었어요.

It was hot, so I sweated.
_____ 땀이 났어요.

It was a little cold so I covered (myself) with a warm blanket.
조금 _____ 따뜻한 이불을 덮었어요.

Since it was a little cold, I covered (myself) with a warm blanket, but then I was hot, so I sweated.
조금 추워서 따뜻한 이불을 _____, 더워서 땀이 났어요.

💬 **왜 땀을 흘렸어요?**
= Why did you sweat?

[   ]
= I covered myself with a blanket, but then I was hot, so I sweated.

💬 **어떤 이불을 덮었어요?**
= What kind of blanket did you cover yourself with?

[   ]
= I covered myself with a warm blanket.

💬 **왜요?**
= Why?

[   ]
= It was a little cold, so I covered myself with a warm blanket.

💬 **그래서 땀을 흘렸어요?**
= That's why you sweated?

네. [   ]
[   ]
= Yes. Since it was a little cold, I covered myself with a warm
  blanket, but then I was hot, so I sweated.

ANSWERS: Speaking Practice

💬 왜 땀을 흘렸어요?
= Why did you sweat?

💬 이불을 덮었는데, 더워서 땀이 났어요.
= I covered myself with a blanket, but then I was hot, so I sweated.

💬 어떤 이불을 덮었어요?
= What kind of blanket did you cover yourself with?

💬 따뜻한 이불을 덮었어요.
= I covered myself with a warm blanket.

💬 왜요?
= Why?

💬 조금 추워서 따뜻한 이불을 덮었어요.
= It was a little cold, so I covered myself with a warm blanket.

💬 그래서 땀을 흘렸어요?
= That's why you sweated?

💬 네. 조금 추워서 따뜻한 이불을 덮었는데, 더워서 땀이 났어요.
= Yes. Since it was a little cold, I covered myself with a warm blanket, but then I was hot, so I sweated.

2 /

급하게 면도하다가 작은 상처가 나서
약을 발라야 돼요.

면도하다
to shave

Present   I shave. =

Past   I shaved. =

Future   I will shave. =

상처
cut, wound

나다
to get

Present   I get (a cut). =

Past   I got (a cut). =

Future   I will get (a cut). =

  ❷ I get a cut. =

  ❷ I got a cut. =

  ❷ I will get a cut. =

약
medicine

바르다
to apply

Present   I apply it. =

Past   I applied it. =

Future   I will apply it. =

  ❷ I apply medicine. =

  ❷ I applied medicine. =

  ❷ I will apply medicine. =

ANSWERS: Conjugation Practice

면도하다

Present | I shave. = 면도해요.

Past | I shaved. = 면도했어요.

Future | I will shave. = 면도할 거예요.

상처

나다

Present | I get (a cut). = 나요.

Past | I got (a cut). = 났어요.

Future | I will get (a cut). = 날 거예요.

❯ I get a cut. = 상처가 나요.

❯ I got a cut. = 상처가 났어요.

❯ I will get a cut. = 상처가 날 거예요.

약

바르다

Present | I apply it. = 발라요.

Past | I applied it. = 발랐어요.

Future | I will apply it. = 바를 거예요.

❯ I apply medicine. = 약을 발라요.

❯ I applied medicine. = 약을 발랐어요.

❯ I will apply medicine. = 약을 바를 거예요.

면도했어요.
I shaved.

상처가 났어요.
I got a cut.

약을 발라요.
I apply medicine.

ADD
급하게

MODIFY
상처 with 작다

CHANGE
the ending with
-아/어/여야 되다

(↓)

급하게 면도했어요.
I shaved in a hurry.

(↓)

작은 상처가 났어요.
I got a small cut.

(↓)

약을 발라야 돼요.
I have to apply medicine.

(↓)

COMBINE
two sentences by using -다가

(↓)

급하게 면도하다가 작은 상처가 났어요.
I got a small cut while I was shaving in a hurry.

(↓)

COMBINE
two sentences by using -아/어/여서

(↓)

급하게 면도하다가 작은 상처가 나서, 약을 발라야 돼요.
I got a small cut while I was shaving in a hurry, so I have to apply medicine.

I shaved.

면도했어요.

I got a cut.

상처가 났어요.

I apply medicine.

약을 발라요.

↓

I shaved in a hurry.

_____ 면도했어요.

↓

I got a small cut.

_____ 상처가 났어요.

↓

I have to apply medicine.

약을 _____.

↓

I got a small cut while I was shaving in a hurry.

급하게 _____ 작은 상처가 났어요.

↓

I got a small cut while I was shaving in a hurry, so I have to apply medicine.

급하게 면도하다가 작은 상처가 _____, 약을 발라야 돼요.

약 있어요?
= Do you have medicine?

💬 왜요?
= Why?

= I have to apply medicine.

💬 다쳤어요?
= Did you get hurt?

= I got a small cut.

💬 뭐 하다가요?
= While doing what?

= I got a small cut while I was shaving in a hurry.

💬 그래서 약이 필요해요?
= So you need medicine?

네.
= Yes. I got a small cut while I was shaving in a hurry, so I have to apply medicine.

ANSWERS: Speaking Practice

💬 약 있어요?
= Do you have medicine?

💬 왜요?
= Why?

💬 약을 발라야 돼요.
= I have to apply medicine.

💬 다쳤어요?
= Did you get hurt?

💬 작은 상처가 났어요.
= I got a small cut.

💬 뭐 하다가요?
= While doing what?

💬 급하게 면도하다가 작은 상처가 났어요.
= I got a small cut while I was shaving in a hurry.

💬 그래서 약이 필요해요?
= So you need medicine?

💬 네. 급하게 면도하다가 작은 상처가 나서 약을 발라야 돼요.
= Yes. I got a small cut while I was shaving in a hurry, so I have to apply medicine.

3

수염이 짧아도 매일 면도해야 돼서
아침에 항상 바빠요.

수염
beard, stubble

짧다
to be short

Present	It is short. =
Past	It was short. =
Future	It will be short. =

❯ One's beard is short. =

❯ One's beard was short. =

❯ One's beard will be short. =

면도하다
to shave

Present	I shave. =
Past	I shaved. =
Future	I will shave. =

바쁘다
to be busy

Present	I am busy. =
Past	I was busy. =
Future	I will be busy. =

ANSWERS: Conjugation Practice

수염

짧다

Present	It is short =	짧아요.
Past	It was short =	짧았어요.
Future	It will be short =	짧을 거예요.

❯ One's beard is short. = 수염이 짧아요.

❯ One's beard was short. = 수염이 짧았어요.

❯ One's beard will be short. = 수염이 짧을 거예요.

면도하다

Present	I shave. =	면도해요.
Past	I shaved. =	면도했어요.
Future	I will shave. =	면도할 거예요.

바쁘다

Present	I am busy. =	바빠요.
Past	I was busy. =	바빴어요.
Future	I will be busy. =	바쁠 거예요.

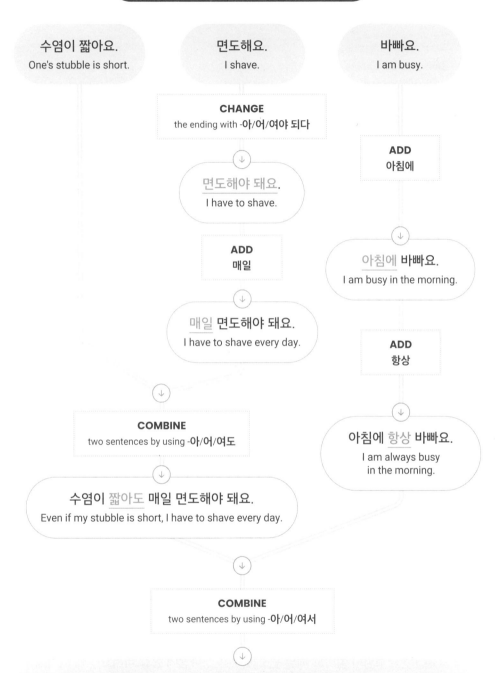

수염이 짧아요.
One's stubble is short.

면도해요.
I shave.

바빠요.
I am busy.

CHANGE
the ending with -아/어/여야 되다

↓

면도해야 돼요.
I have to shave.

ADD
아침에

ADD
매일

↓

매일 면도해야 돼요.
I have to shave every day.

아침에 바빠요.
I am busy in the morning.

ADD
항상

↓

COMBINE
two sentences by using -아/어/여도

↓

아침에 항상 바빠요.
I am always busy
in the morning.

수염이 짧아도 매일 면도해야 돼요.
Even if my stubble is short, I have to shave every day.

↓

COMBINE
two sentences by using -아/어/여서

↓

수염이 짧아도 매일 면도해야 돼서 아침에 항상 바빠요.
Even if my stubble is short, I have to shave every day, so I am always busy in the morning.

One's stubble is short.
수염이 짧아요.

I shave.
면도해요.

I am busy.
바빠요.

I have to shave.
_____.

I am busy in the morning.
_____ 바빠요.

I have to shave every day.
____ 면도해야 돼요.

I am always busy in the morning.
아침에 ____ 바빠요.

Even if my stubble is short, I have to shave every day.
수염이 _____ 매일 면도해야 돼요.

Even if my stubble is short, I have to shave every day, so I am always busy in the morning.
수염이 짧아도 매일 면도해야 ____ 아침에 항상 바빠요.

💬 아침에 면도해요?
= Do you shave in the morning?

네.
= Yes. I shave.

💬 매일이요?
= Every day?

네.
= Yes. I have to shave every day.

💬 수염이 그렇게 빨리 자라요?
= Does your beard grow that fast?

아니요.
= No. Even if I only have a small amount of stubble, I have to shave every day.

💬 진짜요? 아침에 바쁘겠어요.
= Really? You must be busy in the morning.

맞아요.

= That's right. Even if I only have a small amount of stubble, I have to shave every day, so I am always busy in the morning.

ANSWERS: Speaking Practice

💬 아침에 면도해요?
= Do you shave in the morning?

💬 네. 면도해요.
= Yes. I shave.

💬 매일이요?
= Every day?

💬 네. 매일 면도해야 돼요.
= Yes. I have to shave every day.

💬 수염이 그렇게 빨리 자라요?
= Does your beard grow that fast?

💬 아니요. 수염이 짧아도 매일 면도해야 돼요.
= No. Even if I only have a small amount of stubble, I have to shave every day.

💬 진짜요? 아침에 바쁘겠어요.
= Really? You must be busy in the morning.

💬 맞아요. 수염이 짧아도 매일 면도해야 돼서 아침에 항상 바빠요.
= That's right. Even if I only have a small amount of stubble, I have to shave every day, so I am always busy in the morning.

4

다래끼가 더 커지기 전에 집 앞에 있는
안과에 가서 치료를 받으세요.

다래끼
stye

크다
to be big

Present   It is big. =

Past   It was big. =

Future   It will be big. =

❯ A stye is big. =

❯ A stye was big. =

❯ A stye will be big. =

안과
ophthalmologist

가다
to go

Present   I go. =

Past   I went. =

Future   I will go. =

❯ I go to the ophthalmologist. =

❯ I went to the ophthalmologist. =

❯ I will go to the ophthalmologist. =

치료
treatment

받다
to get

Present   I get. =

Past   I got. =

Future   I will get. =

❯ I get treatment. =

❯ I got treatment. =

❯ I will get treatment. =

ANSWERS: Conjugation Practice

✏️ **다래끼**

✏️ **크다**

Present   It is big. = 커요.

Past   It was big. = 컸어요.

Future   It will be big. = 클 거예요.

▶ A stye is big. = 다래끼가 커요.

▶ A stye was big. = 다래끼가 컸어요.

▶ A stye will be big. = 다래끼가 클 거예요.

✏️ **안과**

✏️ **가다**

Present   I go. = 가요.

Past   I went. = 갔어요.

Future   I will go. = 갈 거예요.

▶ I go to the ophthalmologist. = 안과에 가요.

▶ I went to the ophthalmologist. = 안과에 갔어요.

▶ I will go to the ophthalmologist. = 안과에 갈 거예요.

✏️ **치료**

✏️ **받다**

Present   I get. = 받아요.

Past   I got. = 받았어요.

Future   I will get. = 받을 거예요.

▶ I get treatment. = 치료를 받아요.

▶ I got treatment. = 치료를 받았어요.

▶ I will get treatment. = 치료를 받을 거예요.

다래끼가 커요.
A stye is big.

안과에 가요.
I go to the ophthalmologist.

치료를 받아요.
I get treatment.

CHANGE
the ending with
-아/어/여지다

CHANGE
the sentence to
an imperative sentence
using -(으)세요

CHANGE
the sentence to
an imperative sentence
using -(으)세요

↓

↓

↓

다래끼가 커져요.
A stye becomes big.

안과에 가세요.
Go to the ophthalmologist.

치료를 받으세요.
Get treatment.

ADD 더

MODIFY
안과 with 집 앞에 있다

↓

다래끼가 더 커져요.
A stye gets bigger.

↓

집 앞에 있는 안과에 가세요.
Go to the ophthalmologist in front of your house.

↓

COMBINE
two sentences by using -기 전에

↓

다래끼가 더 커지기 전에 집 앞에 있는 안과에 가세요.
Before your stye gets bigger, go to the ophthalmologist in front of your house.

↓

COMBINE
two sentences by using -아/어/여서

↓

다래끼가 더 커지기 전에 집 앞에 있는 안과에 가서 치료를 받으세요.
Before your stye gets bigger, go to the ophthalmologist in front of your house and get treatment.

A stye is big.
다래끼가 커요.

I go to the ophthalmologist.
안과에 가요.

I get treatment.
치료를 받아요.

↓

A stye becomes big.
다래끼가 _____.

Go to the ophthalmologist.
안과에 _____.

Get treatment.
치료를 _____.

↓

A stye gets bigger.
다래끼가 ___ 커져요.

Go to the ophthalmologist in front of your house.
_____ 안과에 가세요.

↓

Before your stye gets bigger, go to the ophthalmologist in front of your house.
다래끼가 더 _____ 집 앞에 있는 안과에 가세요.

↓

Before your stye gets bigger, go to the ophthalmologist in front of your house and get treatment.
다래끼가 더 커지기 전에 집 앞에 있는 안과에 _____ 치료를 받으세요.

💬 다래끼 났어요.
= I have a stye.

= Go to the ophthalmologist.

💬 병원에 가야 돼요?
= Do I have to go to the hospital?

네. 안 그러면
= Yes. Otherwise, the stye will get bigger.

💬 진짜요?
= Really?

네.
= Yes. Go to the ophthalmologist and get treatment.

💬 귀찮아요.
= I am too lazy.

집 앞에 있잖아요.

= It's in front of your house! Before your stye gets bigger, go to the ophthalmologist in front of your house and get treatment.

ANSWERS: Speaking Practice

💬 다래끼 났어요.
= I have a stye.

💬 안과에 가세요.
= Go to the ophthalmologist.

💬 병원에 가야 돼요?
= Do I have to go to the hospital?

💬 네. 안 그러면 다래끼가 커져요.
= Yes. Otherwise, the stye will get bigger.

💬 진짜요?
= Really?

💬 네. 안과에 가서 치료를 받으세요.
= Yes. Go to the ophthalmologist and get treatment.

💬 귀찮아요.
= I am too lazy.

💬 집 앞에 있잖아요. 다래끼가 더 커지기 전에
집 앞에 있는 안과에 가서 치료를 받으세요.
= It's in front of your house! Before your stye gets bigger,
go to the ophthalmologist in front of your house and
get treatment.

5

학교에 늦지 않으려고 서서 양말을
신다가 넘어졌어요.

늦다
to be late

Present   I am late. =

Past   I was late. =

Future   I will be late. =

서다
to stand up

Present   I stand up. =

Past   I stood up. =

Future   I will stand up. =

양말
socks

신다
to put on, to wear

Present   I wear (socks). =

Past   I wore (socks). =

Future   I will wear (socks). =

❯ I wear socks. =

❯ I wore socks. =

❯ I will wear socks. =

넘어지다
to fall over

Present   I fall over. =

Past   I fell over. =

Future   I will fall over. =

ANSWERS: Conjugation Practice

✎ 늦다

   Present   I am late. = 늦어요.

   Past   I was late. = 늦었어요.

   Future   I will be late. = 늦을 거예요.

✎ 서다

   Present   I stand up. = 서요.

   Past   I stood up. = 섰어요.

   Future   I will stand up. = 설 거예요.

✎ 양말

✎ 신다

   Present   I wear (socks). = 신어요.

   Past   I wore (socks). = 신었어요.

   Future   I will wear (socks). = 신을 거예요.

   ❯ I wear socks. = 양말을 신어요.

   ❯ I wore socks. = 양말을 신었어요.

   ❯ I will wear socks. = 양말을 신을 거예요.

✎ 넘어지다

   Present   I fall over. = 넘어져요.

   Past   I fell over. = 넘어졌어요.

   Future   I will fall over. = 넘어질 거예요.

늦어요.
I am late.

서요.
I stand up.

넘어졌어요.
I fell over.

ADD
학교에

양말을 신었어요.
I put on socks.

↓

학교에 늦어요.
I am late for school.

CHANGE
the sentence to the negative form
using -지 않다

COMBINE
two sentences by using
-아/어/여서

↓

서서 양말을 신었어요.
I put on socks standing up.

↓

학교에 늦지 않아요.
I am not late for school.

↓

COMBINE
two sentences by using -(으)려고

↓

학교에 늦지 않으려고 서서 양말을 신었어요.
I put on my socks standing up in order not to be late for school.

↓

COMBINE
two sentences by using -다가

↓

학교에 늦지 않으려고 서서 양말을 신다가 넘어졌어요.
I fell over while I was putting on my socks standing up in order not to be late for school.

I am late.
늦어요.

I stand up.
서요.

I fell over.
넘어졌어요.

I put on socks.
양말을 신었어요.

↓

I am late for school.
_____ 늦어요.

↓

I put on socks standing up.
____ 양말을 신었어요.

I am not late for school.
학교에 _____ .

↓

I put on my socks standing up in order not to be late for school.
학교에 늦지 _____ 서서 양말을 신었어요.

↓

I fell over while I was putting on my socks standing up in order not to be late for school.
학교에 늦지 않으려고 서서 양말을 _____ 넘어졌어요.

넘어졌어요.
= I fell over.

💬 뭐 하다가 넘어졌어요?
= What were you doing when you fell over?

= I fell over while I was putting on my socks.

💬 양말을 어떻게 신었어요?
= How did you put on your socks?

= I put on my socks standing up.

💬 왜요?
= Why?

= I put on my socks standing up in order not to be late for school.

💬 그러다가 넘어졌어요?
= And you fell over while doing it?

네.

= Yes. I fell over while I was putting on my socks standing up in order not to be late for school.

ANSWERS: Speaking Practice

💬 넘어졌어요.
= I fell over.

💬 뭐 하다가 넘어졌어요?
= What were you doing when you fell over?

💬 양말을 신다가 넘어졌어요.
= I fell over while I was putting on my socks.

💬 양말을 어떻게 신었어요?
= How did you put on your socks?

💬 서서 양말을 신었어요.
= I put on my socks standing up.

💬 왜요?
= Why?

💬 학교에 늦지 않으려고 서서 양말을 신었어요.
= I put on my socks standing up in order not to be late for school.

💬 그러다가 넘어졌어요?
= And you fell over while doing it?

💬 네. 학교에 늦지 않으려고 서서 양말을 신다가 넘어졌어요.
= Yes. I fell over while I was putting on my socks standing up in order not to be late for school.

6

물놀이하면 화장이 전부 지워질 것 같으니까 화장품을 챙겨야겠어요.

물놀이하다
to play
in the water

Present — I play in the water. =

Past — I played in the water. =

Future — I will play in the water. =

화장
makeup

지워지다
to come off

Present — (One's makeup) comes off. =

Past — (One's makeup) came off. =

Future — (One's makeup) will come off. =

❯ One's makeup comes off. =

❯ One's makeup came off. =

❯ One's makeup will come off. =

화장품
cosmetics

챙기다
to take, to pack

Present — I take/pack. =

Past — I took/packed. =

Future — I will take/pack. =

❯ I pack my cosmetics. =

❯ I packed my cosmetics. =

❯ I will pack my cosmetics. =

ANSWERS: Conjugation Practice

물놀이하다

Present   I play in the water. = 물놀이해요.

Past   I played in the water. = 물놀이했어요.

Future   I will play in the water. = 물놀이할 거예요.

화장

Present   (One's makeup) comes off. = 지워져요.

지워지다

Past   (One's makeup) came off. = 지워졌어요.

Future   (One's makeup) will come off. = 지워질 거예요.

❯ One's makeup comes off. = 화장이 지워져요.

❯ One's makeup came off. = 화장이 지워졌어요.

❯ One's makeup will come off. = 화장이 지워질 거예요.

화장품

Present   I take/pack. = 챙겨요.

챙기다

Past   I took/packed. = 챙겼어요.

Future   I will take/pack. = 챙길 거예요.

❯ I pack my cosmetics. = 화장품을 챙겨요.

❯ I packed my cosmetics. = 화장품을 챙겼어요.

❯ I will pack my cosmetics. = 화장품을 챙길 거예요.

물놀이해요.
I play in the water.

화장이 지워질 거예요.
My makeup will come off.

화장품을 챙겨요.
I pack my cosmetics.

CHANGE
the ending with
-(으)ㄹ 것 같다

↓

화장이 지워질 것 같아요.
I think my makeup will come off.

COMBINE
two sentences by
using -(으)면

CHANGE
the ending with
-아/어/여야겠다

ADD
전부

↓

화장이 전부 지워질 것 같아요.
I think my makeup will come off
completely.

화장품을 챙겨야겠어요.
I think I should pack my
cosmetics.

↓

물놀이하면 화장이 전부 지워질 것 같아요.
If I play in the water, I think my makeup will
come off completely.

↓

COMBINE
two sentences by using -(으)니까

↓

물놀이하면 화장이 전부 지워질 것 같으니까 화장품을 챙겨야겠어요.
Since I think my makeup will come off completely if I play in the water,
I think I should pack my cosmetics.

I play in the water.

물놀이해요.

My makeup will come off.

화장이 지워질 거예요.

I pack my cosmetics.

화장품을 챙겨요.

I think my makeup will come off.

화장이 _____.

I think my makeup will come off completely.

화장이 _____ 지워질 것 같아요.

I think I should pack my cosmetics.

화장품을 _____.

If I play in the water, I think my makeup will come off completely.

_____ 화장이 전부 지워질 것 같아요.

Since I think my makeup will come off completely if I play in the water, I think I should pack my cosmetics.

물놀이하면 화장이 전부 지워질 것 _____ 화장품을 챙겨야겠어요.

💬 물놀이하러 가요.
  = Let's go play in the water.

좋아요. ⬚
  = Sounds good. I think I will pack my cosmetics.

💬 왜요?
  = Why?

⬚
  = I think my makeup will come off.

💬 많이 지워질까요?
  = Do you think a lot of it will come off?

네. ⬚
  = Yes. I think my makeup will come off completely.

💬 그럴까요?
  = You think so?

네. ⬚
⬚
  = Yes. Since I think my makeup will come off completely if
    I play in the water, I think I should pack my cosmetics.

💬 좋아요. 그럼 가져가요.
  = Okay, then bring them.

ANSWERS: Speaking Practice

💬 물놀이하러 가요.
= Let's go play in the water.

💬 좋아요. 화장품을 챙겨야겠어요.
= Sounds good. I think I will pack my cosmetics.

💬 왜요?
= Why?

💬 화장이 지워질 것 같아요.
= I think my makeup will come off.

💬 많이 지워질까요?
= Do you think a lot of it will come off?

💬 네. 화장이 전부 지워질 것 같아요.
= Yes. I think my makeup will come off completely.

💬 그럴까요?
= You think so?

💬 네. 물놀이하면 화장이 전부 지워질 것 같으니까
화장품을 챙겨야겠어요.
= Yes. Since I think my makeup will come off completely if
I play in the water, I think I should pack my cosmetics.

💬 좋아요. 그럼 가져가요.
= Okay, then bring them.

7 /

아침에 일어나자마자 가볍게 운동하고
시원한 커피를 마신 다음에 회사에 가요.

일어나다
to get up

Present   I get up.　=

Past   I got up.　=

Future   I will get up.　=

운동하다
exercise

Present   I exercise.　=

Past   I exercised.　=

Future   I will exercise.　=

커피
coffee

마시다
to drink

Present   I drink.　=

Past   I drank.　=

Future   I will drink.　=

❯ I drink coffee.　=

❯ I drank coffee.　=

❯ I will drink coffee.　=

가다
to go

Present   I go.　=

Past   I went.　=

Future   I will go.　=

ANSWERS: Conjugation Practice

🖊 **일어나다**   Present   I get up. = 일어나요.

    Past   I got up. = 일어났어요.

    Future   I will get up. = 일어날 거예요.

🖊 **운동하다**   Present   I exercise. = 운동해요.

    Past   I exercised. = 운동했어요.

    Future   I will exercise. = 운동할 거예요.

🖊 **커피**   Present   I drink. = 마셔요.

    Past   I drank. = 마셨어요.

🖊 **마시다**   Future   I will drink. = 마실 거예요.

> ➤ I drink coffee. = 커피를 마셔요.

> ➤ I drank coffee. = 커피를 마셨어요.

> ➤ I will drink coffee. = 커피를 마실 거예요.

🖊 **가다**   Present   I go. = 가요.

    Past   I went. = 갔어요.

    Future   I will go. = 갈 거예요.

일어나요.
I get up.

운동해요.
I exercise.

가요.
I go.

커피를 마셔요.
I drink coffee.

ADD 아침에

ADD 가볍게

↓

아침에 일어나요.
I get up in the morning.

↓

가볍게 운동해요.
I exercise lightly.

MODIFY
커피 with 시원하다

ADD 회사에

↓

COMBINE
two sentences by using -자마자

↓

시원한 커피를 마셔요.
I drink cold coffee.

↓

아침에 일어나자마자 가볍게 운동해요.
As soon as I get up in the morning, I exercise lightly.

↓

회사에 가요.
I go to work.

↓

COMBINE
two sentences by using -고

↓

아침에 일어나자마자 가볍게 운동하고 시원한 커피를 마셔요.
As soon as I get up in the morning, I exercise lightly and drink cold coffee.

↓

COMBINE
two sentences by using -(으)ㄴ 다음에

↓

아침에 일어나자마자 가볍게 운동하고 시원한 커피를 마신 다음에 회사에 가요.
As soon as I get up in the morning, I exercise lightly and drink cold coffee, and then I go to work.

I get up.
일어나요.

I exercise.
운동해요.

I go.
가요.

I drink coffee.
커피를 마셔요.

I get up in the morning.
_____ 일어나요.

I exercise lightly.
_____ 운동해요.

I drink cold coffee.
_____ 커피를 마셔요.

As soon as I get up in the morning, I exercise lightly.
아침에 _____ 가볍게 운동해요.

I go to work.
_____ 가요.

As soon as I get up in the morning, I exercise lightly and drink cold coffee.
아침에 일어나자마자 가볍게 _____ 시원한 커피를 마셔요.

As soon as I get up in the morning, I exercise lightly and drink cold coffee, and then I go to work.
아침에 일어나자마자 가볍게 운동하고 시원한 커피를 _____ 회사에 가요.

💬 아침에 뭐 해요?
= What do you do in the morning?

( )
= I exercise.

💬 진짜요?
= Really?

네. ( )
= Yes. As soon as I get up, I exercise lightly.

💬 그다음에는요?
= And after that?

( )
= I exercise lightly and drink cold coffee.

💬 그리고 회사에 가요?
= And then you go to work?

네. ( )
( )
= Yes. As soon as I get up in the morning, I exercise lightly and drink cold coffee, and then I go to work.

ANSWERS: Speaking Practice

💬 아침에 뭐 해요?
　= What do you do in the morning?

💬 운동해요.
　= I exercise.

💬 진짜요?
　= Really?

💬 네. 아침에 일어나자마자 가볍게 운동해요.
　= Yes. As soon as I get up, I exercise lightly.

💬 그다음에는요?
　= And after that?

💬 가볍게 운동하고 시원한 커피를 마셔요.
　= I exercise lightly and drink cold coffee.

💬 그리고 회사에 가요?
　= And then you go to work?

💬 네. 아침에 일어나자마자 가볍게 운동하고
　시원한 커피를 마신 다음에 회사에 가요.
　= Yes. As soon as I get up in the morning, I exercise
　　lightly and drink cold coffee, and then I go to work.

8

너무 졸렸지만 바로 안 자고
이를 닦은 다음에 침대에 누웠어요.

졸리다
to be sleepy

Present   I am sleepy. =

Past   I was sleepy. =

Future   I will be sleepy. =

자다
to sleep

Present   I sleep. =

Past   I slept. =

Future   I will sleep. =

이
teeth

닦다
to brush

Present   I brush (my teeth). =

Past   I brushed (my teeth). =

Future   I will brush (my teeth). =

❯ I brush my teeth. =

❯ I brushed my teeth. =

❯ I will brush my teeth. =

침대
bed

눕다
to lie

Present   I lie (somewhere). =

Past   I lay (somewhere). =

Future   I will lie (somewhere). =

❯ I lie on the bed. =

❯ I lay on the bed. =

❯ I will lie on the bed. =

ANSWERS: Conjugation Practice

✎ **졸리다**

Present   I am sleepy. = 졸려요.

Past   I was sleepy. = 졸렸어요.

Future   I will be sleepy. = 졸릴 거예요.

✎ **자다**

Present   I sleep. = 자요.

Past   I slept. = 잤어요.

Future   I will sleep. = 잘 거예요.

✎ **이**

Present   I brush (my teeth). = 닦아요.

✎ **닦다**

Past   I brushed (my teeth). = 닦았어요.

Future   I will brush (my teeth). = 닦을 거예요.

❯ I brush my teeth. = 이를 닦아요.

❯ I brushed my teeth. = 이를 닦았어요.

❯ I will brush my teeth. = 이를 닦을 거예요.

✎ **침대**

Present   I lie (somewhere). = 누워요.

Past   I lay (somewhere). = 누웠어요.

✎ **눕다**

Future   I will lie (somewhere). = 누울 거예요.

❯ I lie on the bed. = 침대에 누워요.

❯ I lay on the bed. = 침대에 누웠어요.

❯ I will lie on the bed. = 침대에 누울 거예요.

졸렸어요.
I was sleepy.

잤어요.
I slept.

침대에 누웠어요.
I lay on the bed.

ADD 너무

ADD 바로

이를 닦았어요.
I brushed my teeth.

너무 졸렸어요.
I was so sleepy.

바로 잤어요.
I slept right away.

CHANGE the sentence to the negative form using 안

바로 안 잤어요.
I didn't sleep right away.

COMBINE two sentences by using -지만

너무 졸렸지만 바로 안 잤어요.
I was so sleepy, but I didn't sleep right away.

COMBINE two sentences by using -고

너무 졸렸지만 바로 안 자고 이를 닦았어요.
I was so sleepy, but I didn't sleep right away and I brushed my teeth.

COMBINE two sentences by using -(으)ㄴ 다음에

너무 졸렸지만 바로 안 자고 이를 닦은 다음에 침대에 누웠어요.
I was so sleepy, but I didn't sleep right away and I brushed my teeth before lying on the bed.

I was sleepy.
졸렸어요.

I slept.
잤어요.

I lay on the bed.
침대에 누웠어요.

↓

↓

I brushed my teeth.
이를 닦았어요.

I slept right away.
____ 잤어요.

I was so sleepy.
____ 졸렸어요.

↓

I didn't sleep right away.
바로 _____.

↓

I was so sleepy, but I didn't sleep right away.
너무 _____ 바로 안 잤어요.

↓

I was so sleepy, but I didn't sleep right away and I brushed my teeth.
너무 졸렸지만 바로 안 ____ 이를 닦았어요.

↓

I was so sleepy, but I didn't sleep right away and I brushed my teeth before lying on the bed.
너무 졸렸지만 바로 안 자고 이를 _____ 침대에 누웠어요.

💬 **어제 집에 가니까 피곤했죠?**
= You were tired when you arrived home yesterday, right?

네. _____
= Yes. I was so sleepy.

💬 **바로 잤어요?**
= Did you sleep right away?

아니요. _____
= No. I was so sleepy, but I didn't sleep right away.

💬 **그럼 뭘 했어요?**
= What did you do then?

_____
= I was so sleepy, but I didn't sleep right away and I brushed my teeth.

💬 **그다음에 잤어요?**
= And then you slept?

네. _____
_____
= Yes. I was so sleepy, but I didn't sleep right away and I brushed my teeth before lying on the bed.

ANSWERS: Speaking Practice

💬 어제 집에 가니까 피곤했죠?
= You were tired when you arrived home yesterday, right?

💬 네. 너무 졸렸어요.
= Yes. I was so sleepy.

💬 바로 잤어요?
= Did you sleep right away?

💬 아니요. 너무 졸렸지만 바로 안 잤어요.
= No. I was so sleepy, but I didn't sleep right away.

💬 그럼 뭘 했어요?
= What did you do then?

💬 너무 졸렸지만 바로 안 자고 이를 닦았어요.
= I was so sleepy, but I didn't sleep right away and I brushed my teeth.

💬 그다음에 잤어요?
= And then you slept?

💬 네. 너무 졸렸지만 바로 안 자고 이를 닦은 다음에 침대에 누웠어요.
= Yes. I was so sleepy, but I didn't sleep right away and I brushed my teeth before lying on the bed.

9 /

머리를 안 감으려고 했는데, 갑자기
약속이 생겨서 감아야겠어요.

머리
hair

감다
to wash

Present — I wash (my hair). =

Past — I washed (my hair). =

Future — I will wash (my hair). =

❯ I wash my hair. =

❯ I washed my hair. =

❯ I will wash my hair. =

약속
appointment

생기다
to come up

Present — (Something) comes up. =

Past — (Something) came up. =

Future — (Something) will come up. =

❯ An appointment comes up. =

❯ An appointment came up. =

❯ An appointment will come up. =

ANSWERS: Conjugation Practice

／ **머리**

／ **감다**

Present   I wash (my hair). = 감아요.

Past   I washed (my hair). = 감았어요.

Future   I will wash (my hair). = 감을 거예요.

❯ I wash my hair. = 머리를 감아요.

❯ I washed my hair. = 머리를 감았어요.

❯ I will wash my hair. = 머리를 감을 거예요.

／ **약속**

／ **생기다**

Present   (Something) comes up. = 생겨요.

Past   (Something) came up. = 생겼어요.

Future   (Something) will come up. = 생길 거예요.

❯ An appointment comes up. = 약속이 생겨요.

❯ An appointment came up. = 약속이 생겼어요.

❯ An appointment will come up. = 약속이 생길 거예요.

머리를 감았어요.
I washed my hair.

약속이 생겼어요.
An appointment came up.

감아요.
I wash (my hair).

CHANGE
the sentence to the
negative form using 안

↓

머리를 안 감았어요.
I didn't wash my hair.

CHANGE
the ending with -(으)려고 하다

↓

머리를 안 감으려고 했어요.
I was not going to wash my hair.

ADD
갑자기

↓

갑자기 약속이 생겼어요.
An appointment suddenly
came up.

CHANGE
the ending with
-아/어/여야겠다

↓

감아야겠어요.
I guess I should wash (my hair).

↓

COMBINE
two sentences by using -(으/느)ㄴ데

↓

머리를 안 감으려고 했는데, 갑자기 약속이 생겼어요.
I was not going to wash my hair, but an appointment suddenly came up.

↓

COMBINE
two sentences by using -아/어/여서

↓

머리를 안 감으려고 했는데, 갑자기 약속이 생겨서 감아야겠어요.
I was not going to wash my hair, but an appointment suddenly came up so
I guess I should wash it.

I washed my hair.
머리를 감았어요.

An appointment came up.
약속이 생겼어요.

I wash (my hair).
감아요

↓

↓

I didn't wash my hair.
머리를 _____

An appointment suddenly came up.
_____ 약속이 생겼어요.

↓

↓

I guess I should wash (my hair).
_____.

I was not going to wash my hair.
머리를 안 _____.

↓

I was not going to wash my hair, but an appointment suddenly came up.
머리를 안 감으려고 _____, 갑자기 약속이 생겼어요.

↓

I was not going to wash my hair, but an appointment suddenly came up so I guess I should wash it.
머리를 안 감으려고 했는데, 갑자기 약속이 _____ 감아야겠어요.

💬 머리 감았어요?
= Did you wash your hair?

아니요. ⬚⬚⬚⬚⬚⬚⬚⬚⬚⬚⬚⬚⬚⬚
= No. I didn't wash my hair.

💬 머리 안 감을 거예요?
= Are you not going to wash your hair?

아니요. ⬚⬚⬚⬚⬚⬚⬚⬚⬚⬚⬚⬚⬚⬚
= No. I think I will wash my hair.

💬 왜요?
= Why?

⬚⬚⬚⬚⬚⬚⬚⬚⬚⬚⬚⬚⬚⬚
= An appointment suddenly came up.

💬 그래서 머리를 감을 거예요?
= So you are going to wash your hair?

네. ⬚⬚⬚⬚⬚⬚⬚⬚⬚⬚⬚⬚⬚⬚
⬚⬚⬚⬚⬚⬚⬚⬚⬚⬚⬚⬚⬚⬚
= Yes. I was not going to wash my hair, but an appointment suddenly came up so I guess I should wash it.

ANSWERS: Speaking Practice

💬 머리 감았어요?
= Did you wash your hair?

💬 아니요. 머리(를) 안 감았어요.
= No. I didn't wash my hair.

💬 머리 안 감을 거예요?
= Are you not going to wash your hair?

💬 아니요. 머리(를) 감아야겠어요.
= No. I think I will wash my hair.

💬 왜요?
= Why?

💬 갑자기 약속이 생겼어요.
= An appointment suddenly came up.

💬 그래서 머리를 감을 거예요?
= So you are going to wash your hair?

💬 네. 머리를 안 감으려고 했는데, 갑자기 약속이
생겨서 감아야겠어요.
= Yes. I was not going to wash my hair, but an appointment
suddenly came up so I guess I should wash it.

10

헤어드라이어로 머리를 말리고,
빗으로 빗은 다음에 머리를 묶었어요?

머리
hair

말리다
to dry

Present | I dry it. =

Past | I dried it. =

Future | I will dry it. =

❯ I dry my hair. =

❯ I dried my hair. =

❯ I will dry my hair. =

빗다
to comb

Present | I comb. =

Past | I combed. =

Future | I will comb. =

머리
hair

묶다
to tie

Present | I tie it. =

Past | I tied it. =

Future | I will tie it. =

❯ I tie my hair. =

❯ I tied my hair. =

❯ I will tie my hair. =

ANSWERS: Conjugation Practice

머리

말리다

Present	I dry it.	= 말려요.
Past	I dried it.	= 말렸어요.
Future	I will dry it.	= 말릴 거예요.

❯ I dry my hair. = 머리를 말려요.

❯ I dried my hair. = 머리를 말렸어요.

❯ I will dry my hair. = 머리를 말릴 거예요.

빗다

Present	I comb.	= 빗어요.
Past	I combed.	= 빗었어요.
Future	I will comb.	= 빗을 거예요.

머리

묶다

Present	I tie it.	= 묶어요.
Past	I tied it.	= 묶었어요.
Future	I will tie it.	= 묶을 거예요.

❯ I tie my hair. = 머리를 묶어요.

❯ I tied my hair. = 머리를 묶었어요.

❯ I will tie my hair. = 머리를 묶을 거예요.

머리를 말렸어요.
I dried my hair.

빗었어요.
I combed (my hair).

머리를 묶었어요.
I tied my hair.

ADD
헤어드라이어로

ADD
빗으로

헤어드라이어로 머리를 말렸어요.
I dried my hair with a hairdryer.

빗으로 빗었어요.
I combed (my hair)
with a comb.

COMBINE
two sentences by using -고

헤어드라이어로 머리를 말리고, 빗으로 빗었어요.
I blow-dried my hair and combed it with a comb.

COMBINE
two sentences by using -(으)ㄴ 다음에

헤어드라이어로 머리를 말리고, 빗으로 빗은 다음에 머리를 묶었어요.
After blow-drying my hair and combing it with a comb, I tied my hair up.

CHANGE
the sentence into a question

헤어드라이어로 머리를 말리고, 빗으로 빗은 다음에 머리를 묶었어요?
After blow-drying and combing your hair with a comb, did you tie it up?

I dried my hair.
머리를 말렸어요.

I combed (my hair).
빗었어요.

I tied my hair.
머리를 묶었어요.

I dried my hair with a hairdryer.
_____ 머리를 말렸어요.

I combed (my hair) with a comb.
_____ 빗었어요.

I blow-dried my hair and combed it with a comb.
헤어드라이어로 머리를 _____, 빗으로 빗었어요.

After blow-drying my hair and combing it with a comb, I tied my hair up.
헤어드라이어로 머리를 말리고, 빗으로 _____ 머리를 묶었어요.

After blow-drying and combing your hair with a comb, did you tie it up?
_____ ?

💬 머리 말렸어요?
   = Did you dry your hair?

네. ⬚⬚⬚⬚⬚⬚⬚⬚⬚⬚⬚⬚⬚⬚⬚⬚⬚⬚⬚
   = Yes. I dried my hair with a hairdryer.

💬 그다음에 묶었어요?
   = Did you tie it up after that?

아니요. ⬚⬚⬚⬚⬚⬚⬚⬚⬚⬚⬚⬚⬚⬚⬚
   = No. I dried my hair with a hairdryer and combed it.

💬 뭘로 빗었어요?
   = What did you comb it with?

⬚⬚⬚⬚⬚⬚⬚⬚⬚⬚⬚⬚⬚⬚⬚⬚⬚⬚
   = I combed it with a comb.

💬 그다음에 묶었어요?
   = Did you tie it up after that?

네. ⬚⬚⬚⬚⬚⬚⬚⬚⬚⬚⬚⬚⬚⬚⬚⬚⬚⬚⬚
⬚⬚⬚⬚⬚⬚⬚⬚⬚⬚⬚⬚⬚⬚⬚⬚⬚⬚⬚
   = Yes. After drying my hair with a hairdryer and combing it with a comb, I tied it up.

ANSWERS: Speaking Practice

💬 머리 말렸어요?
= Did you dry your hair?

💬 네. 헤어드라이어로 머리를 말렸어요.
= Yes. I dried my hair with a hairdryer.

💬 그다음에 묶었어요?
= Did you tie it up after that?

💬 아니요. 헤어드라이어로 머리를 말리고 빗었어요.
= No. I dried my hair with a hairdryer and combed it.

💬 뭘로 빗었어요?
= What did you comb it with?

💬 빗으로 빗었어요.
= I combed it with a comb.

💬 그다음에 묶었어요?
= Did you tie it up after that?

💬 네. 헤어드라이어로 머리를 말리고, 빗으로 빗은 다음에 머리를 묶었어요.
= Yes. After drying my hair with a hairdryer and combing it with a comb, I tied it up.

11

머리가 많이 빠져서 비싼 샴푸를 사서
써 봤지만 별로 효과가 없었어요.

머리
hair

빠지다
to fall out

Present   It falls out. =

Past   It fell out. =

Future   It will fall out. =

❯ One's hair falls out. =

❯ One's hair fell out. =

❯ One's hair will fall out. =

샴푸
shampoo

사다
to buy

Present   I buy. =

Past   I bought. =

Future   I will buy. =

❯ I buy shampoo. =

❯ I bought shampoo. =

❯ I will buy shampoo. =

쓰다
to use

Present   I use (something). =

Past   I used (something). =

Future   I will use (something). =

효과
effect

있다
to have, there is

Present   It has (something). =

Past   It had (something). =

Future   It will have (something). =

❯ It has an effect. =

❯ It had an effect. =

❯ It will have an effect. =

ANSWERS: Conjugation Practice

✎ **머리**

✎ **빠지다**

Present	It falls out.	= 빠져요.
Past	It fell out.	= 빠졌어요.
Future	It will fall out.	= 빠질 거예요.

❯ One's hair falls out. = 머리가 빠져요.

❯ One's hair fell out. = 머리가 빠졌어요.

❯ One's hair will fall out. = 머리가 빠질 거예요.

✎ **샴푸**

✎ **사다**

Present	I buy.	= 사요.
Past	I bought.	= 샀어요.
Future	I will buy.	= 살 거예요.

❯ I buy shampoo. = 샴푸를 사요.

❯ I bought shampoo. = 샴푸를 샀어요.

❯ I will buy shampoo. = 샴푸를 살 거예요.

✎ **쓰다**

Present	I use (something).	= 써요.
Past	I used (something).	= 썼어요.
Future	I will use (something).	= 쓸 거예요.

✎ **효과**

✎ **있다**

Present	It has (something).	= 있어요.
Past	It had (something).	= 있었어요.
Future	It will have (something).	= 있을 거예요.

❯ It has an effect. = 효과가 있어요.

❯ It had an effect. = 효과가 있었어요.

❯ It will have an effect. = 효과가 있을 거예요.

머리가 빠졌어요.
My hair fell out.

샴푸를 샀어요.
I bought shampoo.

효과가 있었어요.
It had an effect.

ADD 많이

썼어요.
I used it.

MODIFY
샴푸 with 비싸다

CHANGE
the sentence to the
negative form

머리가 많이 빠졌어요.
A lot of my hair fell out.

CHANGE
the ending with
-아/어/여 보다

비싼 샴푸를 샀어요.
I bought an expensive
shampoo.

효과가 없었어요.
It did not have an effect.

COMBINE
two sentences by using -아/어/여서

써 봤어요.
I tried it.

ADD 별로

머리가 많이 빠져서 비싼 샴푸를 샀어요.
A lot of my hair fell out,
so I bought an expensive shampoo.

별로 효과가 없었어요.
It did not really have an effect.

COMBINE
two sentences by using -아/어/여서

머리가 많이 빠져서 비싼 샴푸를 사서 써 봤어요.
A lot of my hair fell out, so I bought an expensive shampoo and tried it.

COMBINE two sentences by using -지만

머리가 많이 빠져서 비싼 샴푸를 사서 써 봤지만 별로 효과가 없었어요.
A lot of my hair fell out, so I bought an expensive shampoo and tried it,
but it did not really have an effect.

REVIEW: Extension Practice

My hair fell out.
머리가 빠졌어요.

I bought shampoo.
샴푸를 샀어요.

It had an effect.
효과가 있었어요.

I used it.
썼어요.

A lot of my hair fell out.
머리가 ____ 빠졌어요.

I bought an expensive shampoo.
____ 샴푸를 샀어요.

It did not have an effect.
효과가 _____.

I tried it.
_____.

A lot of my hair fell out, so I bought an expensive shampoo.
머리가 많이 _____ 비싼 샴푸를 샀어요.

It did not really have an effect.
____ 효과가 없었어요.

A lot of my hair fell out, so I bought an expensive shampoo and tried it.
머리가 많이 빠져서 비싼 샴푸를 ____ 써 봤어요.

A lot of my hair fell out, so I bought an expensive shampoo and tried it, but it did not really have an effect.
머리가 많이 빠져서 비싼 샴푸를 사서 _____ 별로 효과가 없었어요.

= My hair fell out.

💬 많이요?
= A lot of it?

네.
= Yes. A lot of my hair fell out.

💬 그래서 어떻게 했어요?
= So what did you do?

= I bought an expensive shampoo.

💬 써 봤어요?
= Have you tried it?

네.
= Yes. I bought an expensive shampoo and tried it.

💬 효과가 있었어요?
= Did it have an effect?

아니요.

= No. A lot of my hair fell out, so I bought an expensive shampoo and tried it, but it did not really have an effect.

ANSWERS: Speaking Practice

💬 머리가 빠졌어요.
= My hair fell out.

💬 많이요?
= A lot of it?

💬 네. 머리가 많이 빠졌어요.
= Yes. A lot of my hair fell out.

💬 그래서 어떻게 했어요?
= So what did you do?

💬 비싼 샴푸를 샀어요.
= I bought an expensive shampoo.

💬 써 봤어요?
= Have you tried it?

💬 네. 비싼 샴푸를 사서 써 봤어요.
= Yes. I bought an expensive shampoo and tried it.

💬 효과가 있었어요?
= Did it have an effect?

💬 아니요. 머리가 많이 빠져서 비싼 샴푸를 사서 써 봤지만 별로 효과가 없었어요.
= No. A lot of my hair fell out, so I bought an expensive shampoo and tried it, but it did not really have an effect.

12 /

칫솔을 들기 전에 치약을 많이 짰는데,
제 칫솔이 안 보여서 당황했어요.

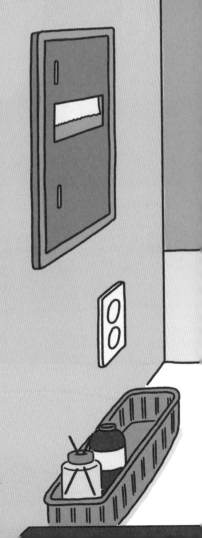

칫솔
toothbrush

들다
to pick up

Present	I pick up. =
Past	I picked up. =
Future	I will pick up. =

❯ I pick up a toothbrush. =

❯ I picked up a toothbrush. =

❯ I will pick up a toothbrush. =

치약
toothpaste

짜다
to squeeze

Present	I squeeze. =
Past	I squeezed. =
Future	I will squeeze. =

❯ I squeeze out the toothpaste. =

❯ I squeezed out the toothpaste. =

❯ I will squeeze out the toothpaste. =

칫솔
toothbrush

보이다
can see,
to be seen,
to be visible

Present	I can see it. =
Past	I could see it. =
Future	It will be seen. / I will be able to see it. =

❯ I can see a toothbrush. =

❯ I could see a toothbrush. =

❯ I will be able to see a toothbrush. =

당황하다
to panic

Present	I panic. =
Past	I panicked. =
Future	I will panic. =

ANSWERS: Conjugation Practice

✎ **칫솔**

Present	I pick up. =	들어요.
Past	I picked up. =	들었어요.

✎ **들다**

Future	I will pick up. =	들 거예요.

❯ I pick up a toothbrush. = 칫솔을 들어요.

❯ I picked up a toothbrush. = 칫솔을 들었어요.

❯ I will pick up a toothbrush. = 칫솔을 들 거예요.

✎ **치약**

Present	I squeeze. =	짜요.
Past	I squeezed. =	짰어요.

✎ **짜다**

Future	I will squeeze. =	짤 거예요.

❯ I squeeze out the toothpaste. = 치약을 짜요.

❯ I squeezed out the toothpaste. = 치약을 짰어요.

❯ I will squeeze out the toothpaste. = 치약을 짤 거예요.

✎ **칫솔**

Present	I can see it. =	보여요.
Past	I could see it. =	보였어요.

✎ **보이다**

Future	It will be seen. / I will be able to see it. =	보일 거예요.

❯ I can see a toothbrush. = 칫솔이 보여요.

❯ I could see a toothbrush. = 칫솔이 보였어요.

❯ I will be able to see a toothbrush. = 칫솔이 보일 거예요.

✎ **당황하다**

Present	I panic. =	당황해요.
Past	I panicked. =	당황했어요.
Future	I will panic. =	당황할 거예요.

치약을 짰어요.
I squeezed out the toothpaste.

칫솔이 보였어요.
I could see a toothbrush.

칫솔을 들었어요.
I picked up a toothbrush.

ADD 많이

MODIFY 칫솔 with 제

당황했어요.
I panicked.

↓

치약을 많이 짰어요.
I squeezed out a lot of toothpaste

제 칫솔이 보였어요.
I could see my toothbrush.

↓

COMBINE
two sentences by using -기 전에

CHANGE
the sentence to the
negative form using 안

↓

칫솔을 들기 전에 치약을 많이 짰어요.
I squeezed out a lot of toothpaste before
picking up my toothbrush.

제 칫솔이 안 보였어요.
I couldn't see my toothbrush
anywhere.

↓

COMBINE two sentences by using -(으/느)ㄴ데
↓

칫솔을 들기 전에 치약을 많이 짰는데, 제 칫솔이 안 보였어요.
I squeezed out a lot of toothpaste before picking up my toothbrush,
but then I couldn't see my toothbrush anywhere.

↓

COMBINE two sentences by using -아/어/여서
↓

칫솔을 들기 전에 치약을 많이 짰는데, 제 칫솔이 안 보여서 당황했어요.
I squeezed out a lot of toothpaste before picking up my toothbrush,
but then I couldn't see my toothbrush anywhere. So, I panicked.

I squeezed out the toothpaste.
치약을 짰어요.

I could see a toothbrush.
칫솔이 보였어요.

I picked up a toothbrush.
칫솔을 들었어요.

(↓)

I panicked.
당황했어요.

(↓)

I squeezed out a lot of toothpaste.
치약을 _____ 짰어요.

I could see my toothbrush.
__ 칫솔이 보였어요.

(↓)

I squeezed out a lot of toothpaste before picking up my toothbrush.
칫솔을 _____ 치약을 많이 짰어요.

(↓)

I couldn't see my toothbrush anywhere.
제 칫솔이 _____.

(↓)

I squeezed out a lot of toothpaste before picking up my toothbrush, but then I couldn't see my toothbrush anywhere.
칫솔을 들기 전에 치약을 많이 _____, 제 칫솔이 안 보였어요.

(↓)

I squeezed out a lot of toothpaste before picking up my toothbrush, but then I couldn't see my toothbrush anywhere. So, I panicked.
칫솔을 들기 전에 치약을 많이 짰는데, 제 칫솔이 안 _____ 당황했어요.

= I panicked.

💬 왜요?
= Why?

= I couldn't see a toothbrush anywhere, so I panicked.

💬 누구 칫솔이요?
= Whose toothbrush?

= I couldn't see my toothbrush anywhere, so I panicked.

💬 그것 때문에 당황했어요?
= You panicked because of that?

그리고
= And I squeezed out a lot of toothpaste.

💬 치약부터 짰어요?
= You squeezed the toothpaste out first?

네.

= Yes. I squeezed out a lot of toothpaste before picking up my toothbrush, but then I couldn't see my toothbrush anywhere. So, I panicked.

ANSWERS: Speaking Practice

💬 당황했어요.
= I panicked.

💬 왜요?
= Why?

💬 칫솔이 안 보여서 당황했어요.
= I couldn't see a toothbrush anywhere, so I panicked.

💬 누구 칫솔이요?
= Whose toothbrush?

💬 제 칫솔이 안 보여서 당황했어요.
= I couldn't see my toothbrush anywhere, so I panicked.

💬 그것 때문에 당황했어요?
= You panicked because of that?

💬 그리고 치약을 많이 짰어요.
= And I squeezed out a lot of toothpaste.

💬 치약부터 짰어요?
= You squeezed the toothpaste out first?

💬 네. 칫솔을 들기 전에 치약을 많이 짰는데, 제 칫솔이 안 보여서
당황했어요.
= Yes. I squeezed out a lot of toothpaste before picking up my toothbrush, but then I couldn't
see my toothbrush anywhere. So, I panicked.

13

양치하려고 컵에 물을 받았는데,
뜨거운 물이 나와서 정말 놀랐어요.

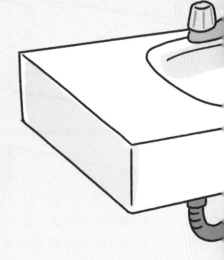

양치하다
to brush one's teeth

Present	I brush my teeth. =
Past	I brushed my teeth. =
Future	I will brush my teeth. =

물
water

받다
to get, to catch, to collect, to fill

Present	I catch. =
Past	I caught. =
Future	I will catch. =

❯ I catch water (in something). =

❯ I caught water (in something). =

❯ I will catch water (in something). =

물
water

나오다
to come out

Present	It comes out. =
Past	It came out. =
Future	It will come out. =

❯ Water comes out. =

❯ Water came out. =

❯ Water will come out. =

놀라다
to be surprised

Present	I am surprised. =
Past	I was surprised. =
Future	I will be surprised. =

ANSWERS: Conjugation Practice

양치하다

Present   I brush my teeth. = 양치해요.

Past   I brushed my teeth. = 양치했어요.

Future   I will brush my teeth. = 양치할 거예요.

물

받다

Present   I catch. = 받아요.

Past   I caught. = 받았어요.

Future   I will catch. = 받을 거예요.

❯ I catch water (in something). = 물을 받아요.

❯ I caught water (in something). = 물을 받았어요.

❯ I will catch water (in something). = 물을 받을 거예요.

물

나오다

Present   It comes out. = 나와요.

Past   It came out. = 나왔어요.

Future   It will come out. = 나올 거예요.

❯ Water comes out. = 물이 나와요.

❯ Water came out. = 물이 나왔어요.

❯ Water will come out. = 물이 나올 거예요.

놀라다

Present   I am surprised. = 놀라요.

Past   I was surprised. = 놀랐어요.

Future   I will be surprised. = 놀랄 거예요.

물을 받았어요.
I caught water (in something).

놀랐어요.
I was surprised.

양치할 거예요.
I will brush my teeth.

ADD
컵에

물이 나왔어요.
Water came out.

↓

컵에 물을 받았어요.
I filled a cup with water.

MODIFY
물 with 뜨겁다

ADD
정말

COMBINE
two sentences by using -(으)려고

↓

뜨거운 물이 나왔어요.
Hot water came out.

↓

양치하려고 컵에 물을 받았어요.
I filled a cup with water to brush my teeth.

↓

정말 놀랐어요.
I was really surprised.

↓

COMBINE
two sentences by using -(으/느)ㄴ데

↓

양치하려고 컵에 물을 받았는데, 뜨거운 물이 나왔어요.
I filled a cup with water to brush my teeth, but hot water came out.

↓

COMBINE
two sentences by using -아/어/여서

↓

양치하려고 컵에 물을 받았는데, 뜨거운 물이 나와서 정말 놀랐어요.
I filled a cup with water to brush my teeth, but hot water came out so I was really surprised.

REVIEW: Extension Practice

I caught water (in something).
물을 받았어요.

I was surprised.
놀랐어요.

I will brush my teeth.
양치할 거예요.

Water came out.
물이 나왔어요.

I filled a cup with water.
_____ 물을 받았어요.

Hot water came out.
_____ 물이 나왔어요.

I filled a cup with water to brush my teeth.
_____ 컵에 물을 받았어요.

I was really surprised.
_____ 놀랐어요.

I filled a cup with water to brush my teeth, but hot water came out.
양치하려고 컵에 물을 _____, 뜨거운 물이 나왔어요.

I filled a cup with water to brush my teeth, but hot water came out
so I was really surprised.
양치하려고 컵에 물을 받았는데, 뜨거운 물이 _____ 정말 놀랐어요.

점점 길어지는 한국어 문장

놀랐어요.

= I was surprised.

💬 **왜요?**

= Why?

= Hot water came out.

💬 **그래서 놀랐어요?**

= That's why you were surprised?

네.

= Yes. I was really surprised that hot water came out.

💬 **왜 물을 틀었어요?**

= Why did you turn on the water?

= I filled a cup with water to brush my teeth.

💬 **그런데 뜨거운 물이 나왔어요?**

= But hot water came out?

네.

= Yes. I filled a cup with water to brush my teeth, but hot water came out so I was really surprised.

ANSWERS: Speaking Practice

💬 놀랐어요.
= I was surprised.

💬 왜요?
= Why?

💬 뜨거운 물이 나왔어요.
= Hot water came out.

💬 그래서 놀랐어요?
= That's why you were surprised?

💬 네. 뜨거운 물이 나와서 정말 놀랐어요.
= Yes. I was really surprised that hot water came out.

💬 왜 물을 틀었어요?
= Why did you turn on the water?

💬 양치하려고 컵에 물을 받았어요.
= I filled a cup with water to brush my teeth.

💬 그런데 뜨거운 물이 나왔어요?
= But hot water came out?

💬 네. 양치하려고 컵에 물을 받았는데, 뜨거운 물이 나와서 정말 놀랐어요.
= Yes. I filled a cup with water to brush my teeth, but hot water came out so I was really surprised.

14/

오랜만에 진하게 화장했더니
어색하지만, 잘 어울리는 것 같아서
기분이 좋아요.

화장하다
to put on
makeup

Present   I put on makeup. =

Past   I put on makeup. =

Future   I will put on makeup. =

어색하다
to feel awkward

Present   I feel awkward. =

Past   I felt awkward. =

Future   I will feel awkward. =

어울리다
to look good on
(someone),
to suit (someone)

Present   It looks good on you. =

Past   It looked good on you. =

Future   It will look good on you. =

기분이 좋다
to feel good

Present   I feel good. =

Past   I felt good. =

Future   I will feel good. =

ANSWERS: Conjugation Practice

화장하다 Present   I put on makeup. = 화장해요.

  Past   I put on makeup. = 화장했어요.

  Future   I will put on makeup. = 화장할 거예요.

어색하다 Present   I feel awkward. = 어색해요.

  Past   I felt awkward. = 어색했어요.

  Future   I will feel awkward. = 어색할 거예요.

어울리다 Present   It looks good on you. = 어울려요.

  Past   It looked good on you. = 어울렸어요.

  Future   It will look good on you. = 어울릴 거예요.

기분이 좋다 Present   I feel good. = 기분이 좋아요.

  Past   I felt good. = 기분이 좋았어요.

  Future   I will feel good. = 기분이 좋을 거예요.

화장했어요.
I put on makeup.

어색해요.
I feel awkward.

어울려요.
It suits me.

기분이 좋아요.
I feel good.

ADD 진하게
↓

진하게 화장했어요.
I put on heavy makeup.

ADD 잘
↓

잘 어울려요.
It really suits me.

ADD 오랜만에
↓

오랜만에 진하게 화장했어요.
I put on heavy makeup
for the first time in a while.

CHANGE
the ending with -는 것 같다
↓

잘 어울리는 것 같아요.
I think it really suits me.

↓

COMBINE two sentences by using -더니
↓

오랜만에 진하게 화장했더니 어색해요.
I feel awkward because I put on heavy makeup
for the first time in a while.

↓

COMBINE two sentences by using -지만
↓

오랜만에 진하게 화장했더니 어색하지만, 잘 어울리는 것 같아요.
I feel awkward because I put on heavy makeup for the first time in a while,
but I think it really suits me.

↓

COMBINE two sentences by using -아/어/여서
↓

오랜만에 진하게 화장했더니 어색하지만, 잘 어울리는 것 같아서 기분이 좋아요.
I feel awkward because I put on heavy makeup for the first time in a while,
but I think it really suits me so I feel good.

I put on makeup
화장했어요.

↓

I put on heavy makeup.
_____ 화장했어요.

↓

I put on heavy makeup
for the first time in a while.
_____ 진하게 화장했어요.

↓

I feel awkward
어색해요.

It suits me.
어울려요.

↓

It really suits me.
___ 어울려요.

↓

I think it really suits me.
잘 _____.

I feel good.
기분이 좋아요.

↓

I feel awkward because I put on heavy makeup
for the first time in a while.
오랜만에 진하게 _____ 어색해요.

↓

I feel awkward because I put on heavy makeup for the first time in a while,
but I think it really suits me.
오랜만에 진하게 화장했더니 _____, 잘 어울리는 것 같아요.

↓

I feel awkward because I put on heavy makeup for the first time in a while,
but I think it really suits me so I feel good.
오랜만에 진하게 화장했더니 어색하지만, 잘 어울리는 것 _____ 기분이 좋아요.

기분이 좋아요.
= I feel good.

💬 **기분 좋아 보여요.**
= Yeah, you do look happy.

> _____

= I put on heavy makeup for the first time in a while.

💬 **예뻐요.**
= You look good.

> _____

= I feel awkward because I put on heavy makeup for the first time in a while.

💬 **잘 어울려요.**
= It really suits you.

고마워요. 저도 _____
= Thank you. I think that it really suits me too.

💬 **그래서 기분이 좋아요?**
= Is that why you are feeling good?

네. _____
_____

= Yes. I feel awkward because I put on heavy makeup for the first time in a while, but I think it really suits me so I feel good.

ANSWERS: Speaking Practice

💬 기분이 좋아요.
= I feel good.

💬 기분 좋아 보여요.
= Yeah, you do look happy.

💬 오랜만에 진하게 화장했어요.
= I put on heavy makeup for the first time in a while.

💬 예뻐요.
= You look good.

💬 오랜만에 진하게 화장했더니 어색해요.
= I feel awkward because I put on heavy makeup for the first time in a while.

💬 잘 어울려요.
= It really suits you.

💬 고마워요. 저도 잘 어울리는 것 같아요.
= Thank you. I think that it really suits me too.

💬 그래서 기분이 좋아요?
= Is that why you are feeling good?

💬 네. 오랜만에 진하게 화장했더니 어색하지만,
잘 어울리는 것 같아서 기분이 좋아요.
= Yes. I feel awkward because I put on heavy makeup for the first time in a while,
but I think it really suits me so I feel good.

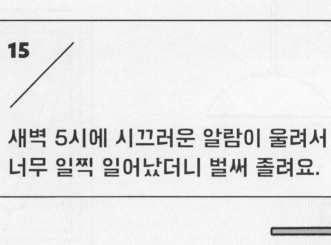

15 /

새벽 5시에 시끄러운 알람이 울려서
너무 일찍 일어났더니 벌써 졸려요.

알람
alarm

울리다
to go off

Present	(The alarm) goes off. =
Past	(The alarm) went off. =
Future	(The alarm) will go off. =

❯ The alarm goes off. =

❯ The alarm went off. =

❯ The alarm will go off. =

일어나다
to wake up

Present	I wake up. =
Past	I woke up. =
Future	I will wake up. =

졸리다
to be sleepy

Present	I am sleepy. =
Past	I was sleepy. =
Future	I will be sleepy. =

ANSWERS: Conjugation Practice

✎ **알람**

✎ **울리다**

Present	(The alarm) goes off. =	울려요.
Past	(The alarm) went off. =	울렸어요.
Future	(The alarm) will go off. =	울릴 거예요.

❯ The alarm goes off. = 알람이 울려요.

❯ The alarm went off. = 알람이 울렸어요.

❯ The alarm will go off. = 알람이 울릴 거예요.

✎ **일어나다**

Present	I wake up. =	일어나요.
Past	I woke up. =	일어났어요.
Future	I will wake up. =	일어날 거예요.

✎ **졸리다**

Present	I am sleepy. =	졸려요.
Past	I was sleepy. =	졸렸어요.
Future	I will be sleepy. =	졸릴 거예요.

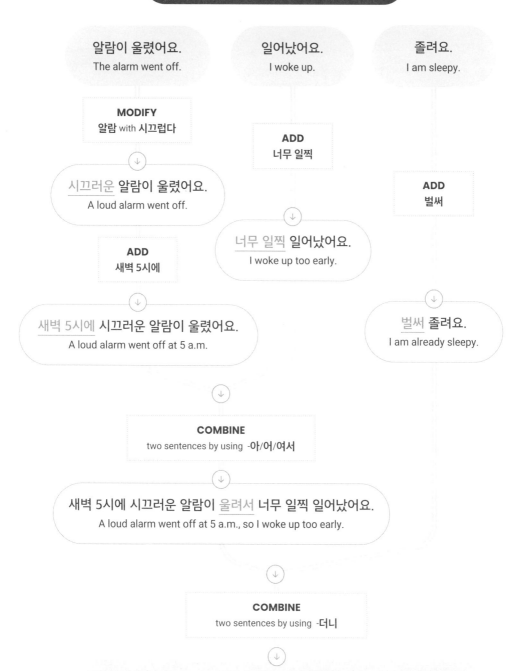

알람이 울렸어요.
The alarm went off.

일어났어요.
I woke up.

졸려요.
I am sleepy.

MODIFY
알람 with 시끄럽다

ADD
너무 일찍

ADD
벌써

시끄러운 알람이 울렸어요.
A loud alarm went off.

너무 일찍 일어났어요.
I woke up too early.

ADD
새벽 5시에

새벽 5시에 시끄러운 알람이 울렸어요.
A loud alarm went off at 5 a.m.

벌써 졸려요.
I am already sleepy.

COMBINE
two sentences by using -아/어/여서

새벽 5시에 시끄러운 알람이 울려서 너무 일찍 일어났어요.
A loud alarm went off at 5 a.m., so I woke up too early.

COMBINE
two sentences by using -더니

새벽 5시에 시끄러운 알람이 울려서 너무 일찍 일어났더니 벌써 졸려요.
A loud alarm went off at 5 a.m., so I woke up too early, and now I am already sleepy.

REVIEW: Extension Practice

The alarm went off.
알람이 울렸어요.

I woke up.
일어났어요.

I am sleepy.
졸려요.

A loud alarm went off.
_____ 알람이 울렸어요.

I woke up too early.
_____ 일어났어요.

I am already sleepy.
____ 졸려요.

A loud alarm went off at 5 a.m.
_____ 시끄러운 알람이 울렸어요.

A loud alarm went off at 5 a.m., so I woke up too early.
새벽 5시에 시끄러운 알람이 _____ 너무 일찍 일어났어요.

A loud alarm went off at 5 a.m., so I woke up too early, and now I am already sleepy.
새벽 5시에 시끄러운 알람이 울려서 너무 일찍 _____ 벌써 졸려요.

벌써 졸려요.
= I am already sleepy.

💬 일찍 일어났어요?
= Did you wake up early?

네.
= Yes. I woke up too early.

💬 언제 일어났어요?
= When did you wake up?

= I woke up at 5 a.m.

💬 왜 그렇게 일찍 일어났어요?
= Why did you wake up so early?

= A loud alarm went off at 5 a.m.

💬 그래서 벌써 졸려요?
= So you are already sleepy?

네.
= Yes. A loud alarm went off, so I woke up too early, and now I am already sleepy.

ANSWERS: Speaking Practice

💬 벌써 졸려요.
= I am already sleepy.

💬 일찍 일어났어요?
= Did you wake up early?

💬 네. 너무 일찍 일어났어요.
= Yes. I woke up too early.

💬 언제 일어났어요?
= When did you wake up?

💬 새벽 5시에 일어났어요.
= I woke up at 5 a.m.

💬 왜 그렇게 일찍 일어났어요?
= Why did you wake up so early?

💬 새벽 5시에 시끄러운 알람이 울렸어요.
= A loud alarm went off at 5 a.m.

💬 그래서 벌써 졸려요?
= So you are already sleepy?

💬 네. 시끄러운 알람이 울려서 너무 일찍 일어났더니 벌써 졸려요.
= Yes. A loud alarm went off, so I woke up too early, and now I am already sleepy.

16 /

제 안경이 너무 더러우니까
쓰기 전에 닦으세요.

안경
glasses

더럽다
to be dirty

Present It is dirty. =

Past It was dirty. =

Future It will be dirty. =

❯ The glasses are dirty. =

❯ The glasses were dirty. =

❯ The glasses will be dirty. =

**(안경을)
쓰다**
to wear,
to put on

Present I wear (glasses). =

Past I wore (glasses). =

Future I will wear (glasses). =

닦다
to polish,
to wipe

Present I polish. =

Past I polished. =

Future I will polish. =

ANSWERS: Conjugation Practice

✏ **안경**

✏ **더럽다**

Present   It is dirty. = 더러워요.

Past   It was dirty. = 더러웠어요.

Future   It will be dirty. = 더러울 거예요.

- ❯ The glasses are dirty. = 안경이 더러워요.

- ❯ The glasses were dirty. = 안경이 더러웠어요.

- ❯ The glasses will be dirty. = 안경이 더러울 거예요.

✏ **(안경을) 쓰다**

Present   I wear (glasses). = 써요.

Past   I wore (glasses). = 썼어요.

Future   I will wear (glasses). = 쓸 거예요.

✏ **닦다**

Present   I polish. = 닦아요.

Past   I polished. = 닦았어요.

Future   I will polish. = 닦을 거예요.

안경이 더러워요.
The glasses are dirty.

써요.
I put on (glasses).

닦아요.
I polish.

MODIFY
안경 with 제

CHANGE
the sentence to the
imperative sentence
using -(으)세요

CHANGE
the sentence to the
imperative sentence
using -(으)세요

제 안경이 더러워요.
My glasses are dirty.

쓰세요.
Put on (glasses).

닦으세요.
Polish.

ADD
너무

제 안경이 너무 더러워요.
My glasses are too dirty.

COMBINE
two sentences by using **-기 전에**

쓰기 전에 닦으세요.
Polish (the glasses) before you put (them) on.

COMBINE
two sentences by using -(으)니까

↓

제 안경이 너무 더러우니까 쓰기 전에 닦으세요.
My glasses are too dirty, so polish them before you put them on.

REVIEW: Extension Practice

The glasses are dirty.
안경이 더러워요.

I put on (glasses).
써요.

I polish.
닦아요.

↓ ↓ ↓

My glasses are dirty.
___ 안경이 더러워요.

Put on (glasses).
_____ .

Polish
_____ .

↓

My glasses are too dirty.
제 안경이 ____ 더러워요.

↓

Polish (the glasses) before you put (them) on.
_____ 닦으세요.

↓

My glasses are too dirty, so polish them before you put them on.
제 안경이 너무 _____ 쓰기 전에 닦으세요.

점점 길어지는 한국어 문장

💬 안경 좀 빌려주세요.
= Lend me your glasses.

= My glasses are dirty.

💬 괜찮아요.
= It's okay.

안 될 것 같아요.
= I don't think so. My glasses are too dirty.

💬 괜찮아요. 빌려주세요.
= It's okay. Lend them to me.

그럼
= Well, then polish them before you put them on.

💬 괜찮아요. 그냥 쓸게요.
= It's okay. I'll just wear them.

안 돼요.

= No way. My glasses are too dirty, so polish them before you put them on.

ANSWERS: Speaking Practice

💬 안경 좀 빌려주세요.
= Lend me your glasses.

💬 안경이 더러워요.
= My glasses are dirty.

💬 괜찮아요.
= It's okay.

💬 안 될 것 같아요. 제 안경이 너무 더러워요.
= I don't think so. My glasses are too dirty.

💬 괜찮아요. 빌려주세요.
= It's okay. Lend them to me.

💬 그럼 쓰기 전에 닦으세요.
= Well, then polish them before you put them on.

💬 괜찮아요. 그냥 쓸게요.
= It's okay. I'll just wear them.

💬 안 돼요. 제 안경이 너무 더러우니까
쓰기 전에 닦으세요.
= No way. My glasses are too dirty, so polish them before
you put them on.

17

새로 생긴 안과에서 시력 검사를
받은 다음에 안경을 맞추려고 하는데
같이 갈래요?

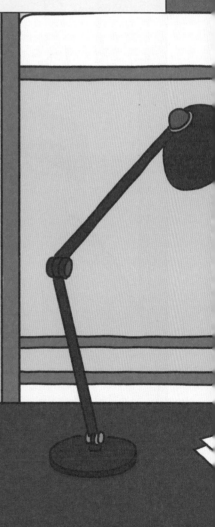

시력 검사
eyesight test

받다
to have

Present   I have (an eyesight test). =

Past   I had (an eyesight test). =

Future   I will have (an eyesight test). =

❯ I have my eyes tested. =

❯ I had my eyes tested. =

❯ I will have my eyes tested. =

안경
glasses

맞추다
to get

Present   I get (glasses). =

Past   I got (glasses). =

Future   I will get (glasses). =

❯ I get a pair of glasses. =

❯ I got a pair of glasses. =

❯ I will get a pair of glasses. =

가다
to go

Present   I go. =

Past   I went. =

Future   I will go. =

ANSWERS: Conjugation Practice

✎ **시력 검사**

✎ **받다**

Present   I **have** (an eyesight test). = 받아요.

Past   I **had** (an eyesight test). = 받았어요.

Future   I **will have** (an eyesight test). = 받을 거예요.

❯ I have my eyes tested. = 시력 검사를 받아요.

❯ I had my eyes tested. = 시력 검사를 받았어요.

❯ I will have my eyes tested. = 시력 검사를 받을 거예요.

✎ **안경**

✎ **맞추다**

Present   I **get** (glasses). = 맞춰요.

Past   I **got** (glasses). = 맞췄어요.

Future   I **will get** (glasses). = 맞출 거예요.

❯ I get a pair of glasses. = 안경을 맞춰요.

❯ I got a pair of glasses. = 안경을 맞췄어요.

❯ I will get a pair of glasses. = 안경을 맞출 거예요.

✎ **가다**

Present   I **go**. = 가요.

Past   I **went**. = 갔어요.

Future   I **will go**. = 갈 거예요.

시력 검사를 받아요.
I have my eyes tested.

CHANGE
the ending with -(으)려고 해요

↓

시력 검사를 받으려고 해요.
I am planning to have my eyes tested.

ADD 안과에서

↓

안과에서 시력 검사를 받으려고 해요.
I am planning to have my eyes tested at the ophthalmology clinic.

MODIFY 안과 with 새로 생기다

↓

새로 생긴 안과에서 시력 검사를 받으려고 해요.
I am planning to have my eyes tested at the newly opened ophthalmology clinic.

안경을 맞춰요.
I get a pair of glasses.

CHANGE
the ending with -(으)려고 해요

↓

안경을 맞추려고 해요.
I am planning to get a pair of glasses.

가요.
I go.

CHANGE
the sentence into a question.

↓

가요?
Will you go?

CHANGE
the ending with -(으)ㄹ래요?

↓

갈래요?
Do you want to go?

ADD 같이

↓

같이 갈래요?
Do you want to go with me?

↓

COMBINE two sentences by using -(으)ㄴ 다음에

↓

새로 생긴 안과에서 시력 검사를 받은 다음에 안경을 맞추려고 해요.
I am planning to get a pair of glasses after having my eyes tested at the newly opened ophthalmology clinic.

↓

COMBINE two sentences by using -(으/느)ㄴ데

↓

새로 생긴 안과에서 시력 검사를 받은 다음에 안경을 맞추려고 하는데 같이 갈래요?
I am planning to get a pair of glasses after having my eyes tested at the newly opened ophthalmology clinic. Do you want to go with me?

REVIEW: Extension Practice

I have my eyes tested.
시력 검사를 받아요.

I get a pair of glasses.
안경을 맞춰요.

I go.
가요.

↓

I am planning to have my eyes tested.
시력 검사를 _____.

↓

Will you go?
_____?

↓

I am planning to get a pair of glasses.
안경을 _____.

↓

I am planning to have my eyes tested at the ophthalmology clinic.
_____ 시력 검사를 받으려고 해요.

Do you want to go?
_____?

↓

I am planning to have my eyes tested at the newly opened ophthalmology clinic.
_____ 안과에서 시력 검사를 받으려고 해요.

Do you want to go with me?
_____ 갈래요?

↓

I am planning to get a pair of glasses after having my eyes tested at the newly opened ophthalmology clinic.
새로 생긴 안과에서 시력 검사를 _____ 안경을 맞추려고 해요.

↓

I am planning to get a pair of glasses after having my eyes tested at the newly opened ophthalmology clinic. Do you want to go with me?
새로 생긴 안과에서 시력 검사를 받은 다음에 안경을 맞추려고 _____ 같이 갈래요?

💬 눈이 나빠졌어요?
= Have your eyes gotten bad?

네.
= Yes. So I am planning to have my eyes tested.

💬 어디에서요?
= Where?

= I am planning to have my eyes tested at the newly opened ophthalmology clinic.

💬 안경 쓰려고요?
= Are you going to wear glasses?

네.
= Yes. I am planning to get a pair of glasses.

💬 언제 갈 거예요?
= When are you going?

내일이요.

= Tomorrow. I am planning to get a pair of glasses after having my eyes tested at the newly opened ophthalmology clinic. Do you want to go with me?

ANSWERS: Speaking Practice

💬 눈이 나빠졌어요?
= Have your eyes gotten bad?

💬 네. 그래서 시력 검사를 받으려고 해요.
= Yes. So I am planning to have my eyes tested.

💬 어디에서요?
= Where?

💬 새로 생긴 안과에서 시력 검사를 받으려고 해요.
= I am planning to have my eyes tested at the newly opened ophthalmology clinic.

💬 안경 쓰려고요?
= Are you going to wear glasses?

💬 네. 안경을 맞추려고 해요.
= Yes. I am planning to get a pair of glasses.

💬 언제 갈 거예요?
= When are you going?

💬 내일이요. 새로 생긴 안과에서 시력 검사를 받은 다음에 안경을 맞추려고 하는데 같이 갈래요?
= Tomorrow. I am planning to get a pair of glasses after having my eyes tested at the newly opened ophthalmology clinic. Do you want to go with me?

18 /

시간이 없어서 오래된 마스카라를
대충 발랐더니 다 번졌어요.

시간
time

있다
to have,
there is

Present I have (something). =

Past I had (something). =

Future I will have (something). =

❯ I have time. =

❯ I had time. =

❯ I will have time. =

마스카라
mascara

바르다
to apply

Present I apply it. =

Past I applied it. =

Future I will apply it. =

❯ I apply mascara. =

❯ I applied mascara. =

❯ I will apply mascara. =

번지다
to be smudged

Present It gets smudged. =

Past It got smudged. / It has been smudged. =

Future It will get smudged. =

ANSWERS: Conjugation Practice

⟋ **시간**

⟋ **있다**

Present	I have (something). =	있어요.
Past	I had (something). =	있었어요.
Future	I will have (something). =	있을 거예요.

❯ I have time. = 시간이 있어요.

❯ I had time. = 시간이 있었어요.

❯ I will have time. = 시간이 있을 거예요.

⟋ **마스카라**

⟋ **바르다**

Present	I apply it. =	발라요.
Past	I applied it. =	발랐어요.
Future	I will apply it. =	바를 거예요.

❯ I apply mascara. = 마스카라를 발라요.

❯ I applied mascara. = 마스카라를 발랐어요.

❯ I will apply mascara. = 마스카라를 바를 거예요.

⟋ **번지다**

Present	It gets smudged. =	번져요.
Past	It got smudged. / It has been smudged. =	번졌어요.
Future	It will get smudged. =	번질 거예요.

시간이 있었어요.
I had time.

마스카라를 발랐어요.
I applied mascara.

번졌어요.
It got smudged.

MODIFY
마스카라 with 오래되다

CHANGE
the sentence to
the negative form

오래된 마스카라를 발랐어요.
I applied my old mascara.

ADD
다

시간이 없었어요.
I didn't have time.

ADD
대충

오래된 마스카라를 대충 발랐어요.
I cursorily applied my old mascara.

다 번졌어요.
It all got smudged.

COMBINE
two sentences by using -아/어/여서

시간이 없어서 오래된 마스카라를 대충 발랐어요.
I didn't have time, so I cursorily applied my old mascara.

COMBINE
two sentences by using -더니

시간이 없어서 오래된 마스카라를 대충 발랐더니 다 번졌어요.
I didn't have time, so I cursorily applied my old mascara, and it all got smudged.

I had time.
시간이 있었어요.

I applied mascara.
마스카라를 발랐어요.

It got smudged.
번졌어요.

I applied my old mascara.
_____ 마스카라를 발랐어요.

I didn't have time.
시간이 _____.

I cursorily applied my old mascara.
오래된 마스카라를 ____ 발랐어요.

It all got smudged.
___ 번졌어요.

I didn't have time, so I cursorily applied my old mascara.
시간이 _____ 오래된 마스카라를 대충 발랐어요.

I didn't have time, so I cursorily applied my old mascara, and it all got smudged.
시간이 없어서 오래된 마스카라를 대충 _____ 다 번졌어요.

마스카라가 다 번졌어요.

= My mascara has all been smudged.

 어떤 마스카라를 발랐어요?

= What mascara did you apply?

= I applied my old mascara.

💬 마스카라를 어떻게 발랐어요?

= How did you apply it?

= I cursorily applied it.

💬 왜 대충 발랐어요?

= Why did you cursorily apply it?

= I didn't have time, so I cursorily applied it.

💬 그래서 다 번졌어요?

= So it all got smudged?

네.

= Yes. I didn't have time, so I cursorily applied my old mascara, and it all got smudged.

ANSWERS: Speaking Practice

💬 마스카라가 다 번졌어요.
= My mascara has all been smudged.

💬 어떤 마스카라를 발랐어요?
= What mascara did you apply?

💬 오래된 마스카라를 발랐어요.
= I applied my old mascara.

💬 마스카라를 어떻게 발랐어요?
= How did you apply it?

💬 대충 발랐어요.
= I cursorily applied it.

💬 왜 대충 발랐어요?
= Why did you cursorily apply it?

💬 시간이 없어서 대충 발랐어요.
= I didn't have time, so I cursorily applied it.

💬 그래서 다 번졌어요?
= So it all got smudged?

💬 네. 시간이 없어서 오래된 마스카라를 대충 발랐더니 다 번졌어요.
= Yes. I didn't have time, so I cursorily applied my old mascara, and it all got smudged.

19 /

너무 밝아서 두꺼운 커튼을 치니까
어두워졌어요.

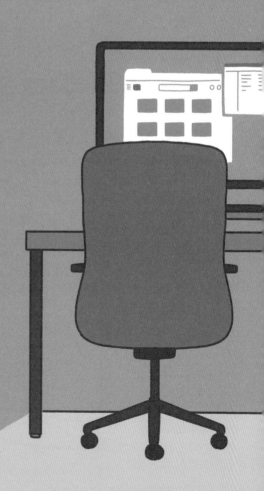

밝다
to be bright

Present   It is bright. =

Past   It was bright. =

Future   It will be bright. =

커튼
curtain

치다
to draw,
to close

Present   I close (the curtains) =

Past   I closed (the curtains). =

Future   I will close (the curtains). =

❯ I close the curtains. =

❯ I closed the curtains. =

❯ I will close the curtains. =

어둡다
to be dark

Present   It is dark. =

Past   It was dark. =

Future   It will be dark. =

ANSWERS: Conjugation Practice

밝다

Present   It is bright. = 밝아요.

Past   It was bright. = 밝았어요.

Future   It will be bright. = 밝을 거예요.

커튼

치다

Present   I close (the curtains) = 쳐요.

Past   I closed (the curtains). = 쳤어요.

Future   I will close (the curtains). = 칠 거예요.

▶ I close the curtains. = 커튼을 쳐요.

▶ I closed the curtains. = 커튼을 쳤어요.

▶ I will close the curtains. = 커튼을 칠 거예요.

어둡다

Present   It is dark. = 어두워요.

Past   It was dark. = 어두웠어요.

Future   It will be dark. = 어두울 거예요.

밝았어요.
It was bright.

커튼을 쳤어요.
I closed the curtains.

어두웠어요.
It was dark.

ADD
너무

MODIFY
커튼 with 두껍다

↓
너무 밝았어요.
It was too bright.

↓
두꺼운 커튼을 쳤어요.
I closed the heavy curtains.

CHANGE
the ending with -아/어/여지다

↓
COMBINE
two sentences by using -아/어/여서

↓
어두워졌어요.
It has become dark.

↓
너무 밝아서 두꺼운 커튼을 쳤어요.
It was too bright, so I closed the heavy curtains.

↓
COMBINE
two sentences by using -(으)니까

↓
너무 밝아서 두꺼운 커튼을 치니까 어두워졌어요.
Since it was too bright, I closed the heavy curtains, so it has become dark.

REVIEW: Extension Practice

It was bright.
밝았어요.

I closed the curtains.
커튼을 쳤어요.

It was dark.
어두웠어요.

It was too bright.
_____ 밝았어요.

I closed the heavy curtains.
_____ 커튼을 쳤어요.

It has become dark.
_____.

It was too bright, so I closed the heavy curtains.
너무 _____ 두꺼운 커튼을 쳤어요.

Since it was too bright, I closed the heavy curtains, so it has become dark.
너무 밝아서 두꺼운 커튼을 _____ 어두워졌어요.

커튼을 쳤어요.
= I closed the curtains.

💬 **왜요?**
= Why?

⬭

= It was too bright.

💬 **그래서 커튼을 쳤어요?**
= So you closed the curtains?

네. ⬭
= Yes. It was too bright, so I closed the curtains.

💬 **어떤 커튼을 쳤어요?**
= Which curtains did you close?

⬭

= I closed the heavy curtains.

💬 **이제 어두워요?**
= Is it dark now?

네. ⬭
= Yes. It has become dark because I closed the heavy curtains.

ANSWERS: Speaking Practice

💬 커튼을 쳤어요.
= I closed the curtains.

💬 왜요?
= Why?

💬 너무 밝았어요.
= It was too bright.

💬 그래서 커튼을 쳤어요?
= So you closed the curtains?

💬 네. 너무 밝아서 커튼을 쳤어요.
= Yes. It was too bright, so I closed the curtains.

💬 어떤 커튼을 쳤어요?
= Which curtains did you close?

💬 두꺼운 커튼을 쳤어요.
= I closed the heavy curtains.

💬 이제 어두워요?
= Is it dark now?

💬 네. 두꺼운 커튼을 치니까 어두워졌어요.
= Yes. It has become dark because I closed the heavy curtains.

20 /

어두워지기 전에 다시 나갈 건데
왜 겉에 입은 옷을 벗었어요?

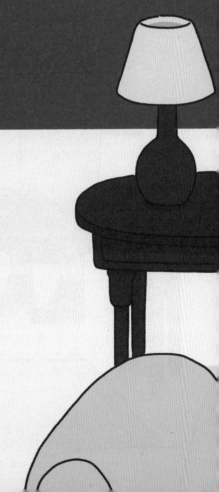

어둡다
to be dark

Present   It is dark.   =

Past   It was dark.   =

Future   It will be dark.   =

나가다
to go out

Present   I go out.   =

Past   I went out.   =

Future   I will go out.   =

옷
clothes

벗다
to take off

Present   I take off (something).   =

Past   I took off (something).   =

Future   I will take off (something).   =

❯ I take off my clothes.   =

❯ I took off my clothes.   =

❯ I will take off my clothes.   =

ANSWERS: Conjugation Practice

어둡다

Present It is dark. = 어두워요.

Past It was dark. = 어두웠어요.

Future It will be dark. = 어두울 거예요.

나가다

Present I go out. = 나가요.

Past I went out. = 나갔어요.

Future I will go out. = 나갈 거예요.

옷

벗다

Present I take off (something). = 벗어요.

Past I took off (something). = 벗었어요.

Future I will take off (something). = 벗을 거예요.

❯ I take off my clothes. = 옷을 벗어요.

❯ I took off my clothes. = 옷을 벗었어요.

❯ I will take off my clothes. = 옷을 벗을 거예요.

어두워요.
It is dark.

CHANGE
the ending with -아/어/여지다

↓

어두워져요.
It becomes dark.

나갈 거예요.
We will go out.

ADD
다시

↓

다시 나갈 거예요.
We will go out again.

옷을 벗었어요.
I took off my clothes.

CHANGE
the sentence into a question

↓

옷을 벗었어요?
Did you take off your clothes?

MODIFY
옷 with 겉에 입다

↓

겉에 입은 옷을 벗었어요?
Did you take off your outerwear?

ADD
왜

↓

왜 겉에 입은 옷을 벗었어요?
Why did you take off your outerwear?

↓

COMBINE
two sentences by using -기 전에

↓

어두워지기 전에 다시 나갈 거예요.
We will go out again before it becomes dark.

↓

COMBINE
two sentences by using -(으/느)ㄴ데

↓

어두워지기 전에 다시 나갈 건데 왜 겉에 입은 옷을 벗었어요?
We will go out again before it becomes dark, so why did you take off your outerwear?

REVIEW: Extension Practice

It is dark.
어두워요.

We will go out.
나갈 거예요.

I took off my clothes.
옷을 벗었어요.

It becomes dark.
_____.

We will go out again.
____ 나갈 거예요.

Did you take off your clothes?
_____?

Did you take off your outerwear?
_____ 옷을 벗었어요?

We will go out again before it becomes dark.
_____ 다시 나갈 거예요.

Why did you take off your outerwear?
__ 겉에 입은 옷을 벗었어요?

We will go out again before it becomes dark, so why did you take off your outerwear?
어두워지기 전에 다시 나갈 ____ 왜 겉에 입은 옷을 벗었어요?

_____

= Did you take off your clothes?

💬 네? 어떤 옷이요?

= What? Which clothes?

_____

= Did you take off your outerwear?

💬 아, 네. 왜요?

= Oh, yes. Why?

우리 _____

= We will go out again.

💬 아, 진짜요?

= Oh, really?

네. _____

= Yes. We will go out again before it becomes dark, so why did you take off your outerwear?

💬 몰랐어요.

= I didn't know.

ANSWERS: Speaking Practice

💬 옷을 벗었어요?
= Did you take off your clothes?

💬 네? 어떤 옷이요?
= What? Which clothes?

💬 겉에 입은 옷을 벗었어요?
= Did you take off your outerwear?

💬 아, 네. 왜요?
= Oh, yes. Why?

💬 우리 다시 나갈 거예요.
= We will go out again.

💬 아, 진짜요?
= Oh, really?

💬 네. 어두워지기 전에 다시 나갈 건데 왜 겉에 입은 옷을 벗었어요?
= Yes. We will go out again before it becomes dark, so why did you take off your outerwear?

💬 몰랐어요.
= I didn't know.

21 /

친구를 만나기 전에
얼른 번진 화장을 고쳐야겠어요.

친구
friend

만나다
to meet

Present   I meet. =

Past   I met. =

Future   I will meet. =

❯ I meet my friend. =

❯ I met my friend. =

❯ I will meet my friend. =

화장
makeup

고치다
to fix

Present   I fix it. =

Past   I fixed it. =

Future   I will fix it. =

❯ I fix my makeup. =

❯ I fixed my makeup. =

❯ I will fix my makeup. =

ANSWERS: Conjugation Practice

친구

만나다

Present   I meet. = 만나요.

Past   I met. = 만났어요.

Future   I will meet. = 만날 거예요.

- ❯ I meet my friend. = 친구를 만나요.

- ❯ I met my friend. = 친구를 만났어요.

- ❯ I will meet my friend. = 친구를 만날 거예요.

화장

고치다

Present   I fix it. = 고쳐요.

Past   I fixed it. = 고쳤어요.

Future   I will fix it. = 고칠 거예요.

- ❯ I fix my makeup. = 화장을 고쳐요.

- ❯ I fixed my makeup. = 화장을 고쳤어요.

- ❯ I will fix my makeup. = 화장을 고칠 거예요.

친구를 만나요.
I meet my friend.

화장을 고쳐요.
I fix my makeup.

MODIFY
화장 with 번지다

↓

<u>번진</u> 화장을 고쳐요.
I fix my smudged makeup.

CHANGE
the ending with -아/어/여야겠다

↓

번진 화장을 <u>고쳐야겠어요</u>.
I guess I should fix my smudged makeup.

ADD
얼른

↓

<u>얼른</u> 번진 화장을 고쳐야겠어요.
I guess I should fix my smudged makeup quickly.

COMBINE
two sentences by using -기 전에

친구를 <u>만나기 전에</u> 얼른 번진 화장을 고쳐야겠어요.
Before meeting my friend, I guess I should fix my smudged makeup quickly.

REVIEW: Extension Practice

I meet my friend.
친구를 만나요.

I fix my makeup.
화장을 고쳐요.

↓

I fix my smudged makeup.
____ 화장을 고쳐요.

↓

I guess I should fix my smudged makeup.
번진 화장을 _____.

↓

I guess I should fix my smudged makeup quickly.
____ 번진 화장을 고쳐야겠어요.

↓

Before meeting my friend, I guess I should fix my smudged makeup quickly.
친구를 _____ 얼른 번진 화장을 고쳐야겠어요.

💬 화장이 번졌어요.
  = Your makeup has been smudged.

아, 그래요?
  = Oh, has it? I guess I should fix my makeup.

💬 약속 있어요?
  = Are you going to meet someone?

네.
  = Yes. I'm meeting my friend.

💬 그럼 얼른 고쳐요.
  = Then hurry and fix it.

네.
  = Yes. I guess I should fix my smudged makeup quickly.

💬 친구 언제 만나요?
  = When are you meeting your friend?

곧이요.

  = Soon. Before meeting my friend,
    I guess I should fix my smudged makeup quickly.

💬 화장이 번졌어요.
= Your makeup has been smudged.

💬 아, 그래요? 화장을 고쳐야겠어요.
= Oh, has it? I guess I should fix my makeup.

💬 약속 있어요?
= Are you going to meet someone?

💬 네. 친구를 만나요.
= Yes. I'm meeting my friend.

💬 그럼 얼른 고쳐요.
= Then hurry and fix it.

💬 네. 얼른 번진 화장을 고쳐야겠어요.
= Yes. I guess I should fix my smudged makeup quickly.

💬 친구 언제 만나요?
= When are you meeting your friend?

💬 곧이요. 친구를 만나기 전에 얼른 번진 화장을 고쳐야겠어요.
= Soon. Before meeting my friend,
  I guess I should fix my smudged makeup quickly.

22 /

아침에 면도해도 저녁이 되면 수염이
또 자라니까 한 번 더 면도해야 돼요.

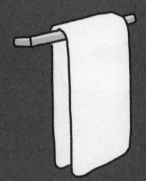

면도하다
to shave

Present   I shave. =

Past   I shaved. =

Future   I will shave. =

저녁
evening

되다
to become

Present   It becomes. =

Past   It became. =

Future   It will become. =

❯ It becomes evening. =

❯ It has become evening. =

❯ It will become evening. =

수염
beard, stubble

자라다
to grow

Present   It grows. =

Past   It grew. =

Future   It will grow. =

❯ My beard grows. =

❯ My beard grew. =

❯ My beard will grow. =

ANSWERS: Conjugation Practice

면도하다

Present   I shave. = 면도해요.

Past   I shaved. = 면도했어요.

Future   I will shave. = 면도할 거예요.

저녁

Present   It becomes. = 돼요.

되다

Past   It became. = 됐어요.

Future   It will become. = 될 거예요.

❯ It becomes evening. = 저녁이 돼요.

❯ It has become evening. = 저녁이 됐어요.

❯ It will become evening. = 저녁이 될 거예요.

수염

Present   It grows. = 자라요.

자라다

Past   It grew. = 자랐어요.

Future   It will grow. = 자랄 거예요.

❯ My beard grows. = 수염이 자라요.

❯ My beard grew. = 수염이 자랐어요.

❯ My beard will grow. = 수염이 자랄 거예요.

면도해요.
I shave.

저녁이 돼요.
It becomes evening.

수염이 자라요.
My beard grows.

면도해요.
I shave.

ADD 또

ADD 아침에

ADD 한 번 더

수염이 또 자라요.
My beard grows again.

아침에 면도해요.
I shave in the morning.

한 번 더 면도해요.
I shave one more time.

COMBINE
two sentences by using -(으)면

저녁이 되면 수염이 또 자라요.
By the time it is evening,
my beard has grown out again.

CHANGE
the ending with
-아/어/여야 되다

COMBINE
two sentences by using -아/어/여도

한 번 더 면도해야 돼요.
I need to shave one more time.

아침에 면도해도 저녁이 되면 수염이 또 자라요.
Even if I shave in the morning, by the time it is evening,
my beard has grown out again.

COMBINE
two sentences by using -(으)니까

아침에 면도해도 저녁이 되면 수염이 또 자라니까 한 번 더 면도해야 돼요.
Even if I shave in the morning, by the time it is evening,
my beard has grown out again. So, I need to shave one more time.

REVIEW: Extension Practice

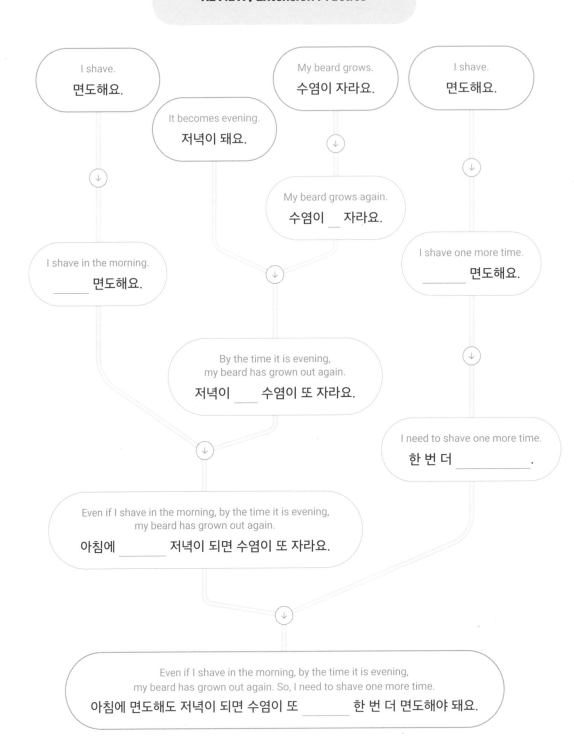

I shave.
면도해요.

It becomes evening.
저녁이 돼요.

My beard grows.
수염이 자라요.

I shave.
면도해요.

My beard grows again.
수염이 ___ 자라요.

I shave in the morning.
_____ 면도해요.

I shave one more time.
_____ 면도해요.

By the time it is evening,
my beard has grown out again.
저녁이 ____ 수염이 또 자라요.

I need to shave one more time.
한 번 더 _____.

Even if I shave in the morning, by the time it is evening,
my beard has grown out again.
아침에 _____ 저녁이 되면 수염이 또 자라요.

Even if I shave in the morning, by the time it is evening,
my beard has grown out again. So, I need to shave one more time.
아침에 면도해도 저녁이 되면 수염이 또 _____ 한 번 더 면도해야 돼요.

💬 면도 안 했어요?
= Have you not shaved?

= I shaved in the morning.

💬 그래요? 근데 수염이 벌써 자랐어요?
= You did? But your beard has grown out already?

네.
= Yes. By the time it is evening, my beard has grown out again.

💬 우와! 빨리 자란다.
= Wow! It grows so fast.

네. 그래서
= Yes. So I need to shave one more time.

💬 저녁에 한 번 더요?
= One more time in the evening?

네.

= Yes. Even if I shave in the morning, by the time it is evening,
  my beard has grown out again. So, I need to shave one more time.

ANSWERS: Speaking Practice

💬 면도 안 했어요?
= Have you not shaved?

💬 아침에 면도했어요.
= I shaved in the morning.

💬 그래요? 근데 수염이 벌써 자랐어요?
= You did? But your beard has grown out already?

💬 네. 저녁이 되면 수염이 또 자라요.
= Yes. By the time it is evening, my beard has grown out again.

💬 우와! 빨리 자란다.
= Wow! It grows so fast.

💬 네. 그래서 한 번 더 면도해야 돼요.
= Yes. So I need to shave one more time.

💬 저녁에 한 번 더요?
= One more time in the evening?

💬 네. 아침에 면도해도 저녁이 되면
수염이 또 자라니까 한 번 더 면도해야 돼요.
= Yes. Even if I shave in the morning, by the time it is evening,
my beard has grown out again. So, I need to shave one more
time.

23

눈이 너무 안 좋아서 텔레비전을
보려면 안경을 써야 해요.

눈
eye, eyesight

좋다
to be good

Present	It is good. =
Past	It was good. =
Future	It will be good. =

❯ One's eyesight is good. =

❯ One's eyesight was good. =

❯ One's eyesight will be good. =

텔레비전
television

보다
to watch

Present	I watch. =
Past	I watched. =
Future	I will watch. =

❯ I watch television. =

❯ I watched television. =

❯ I will watch television. =

안경
glasses

쓰다
to put on,
to wear

Present	I wear (glasses). =
Past	I wore (glasses). =
Future	I will wear (glasses). =

❯ I wear glasses. =

❯ I wore glasses. =

❯ I will wear glasses. =

ANSWERS: Conjugation Practice

눈

좋다

Present	It is good.	= 좋아요.
Past	It was good.	= 좋았어요.
Future	It will be good.	= 좋을 거예요.

❯ One's eyesight is good. = 눈이 좋아요.

❯ One's eyesight was good. = 눈이 좋았어요.

❯ One's eyesight will be good. = 눈이 좋을 거예요.

텔레비전

보다

Present	I watch.	= 봐요.
Past	I watched.	= 봤어요.
Future	I will watch.	= 볼 거예요.

❯ I watch television. = 텔레비전을 봐요.

❯ I watched television. = 텔레비전을 봤어요.

❯ I will watch television. = 텔레비전을 볼 거예요.

안경

쓰다

Present	I wear (glasses).	= 써요.
Past	I wore (glasses).	= 썼어요.
Future	I will wear (glasses).	= 쓸 거예요.

❯ I wear glasses. = 안경을 써요.

❯ I wore glasses. = 안경을 썼어요.

❯ I will wear glasses. = 안경을 쓸 거예요.

눈이 좋아요.
I have good eyesight.

텔레비전을 봐요.
I watch TV.

안경을 써요.
I wear glasses.

CHANGE
the sentence to the
negative form using 안

CHANGE
the ending with
-아/어/여야 하다

↓

눈이 안 좋아요.
I have bad eyesight.

↓

안경을 써야 해요.
I have to wear glasses.

ADD
너무

↓

COMBINE
two sentences by using -(으)려면

↓

눈이 너무 안 좋아요.
I have really bad eyesight.

↓

텔레비전을 보려면 안경을 써야 해요.
If I want to watch TV, I have to wear glasses.

↓

COMBINE
two sentences by using -아/어/여서

↓

눈이 너무 안 좋아서 텔레비전을 보려면 안경을 써야 해요.
I have really bad eyesight, so I have to wear glasses if I want to watch TV.

I have good eyesight.
눈이 좋아요.

I watch TV.
텔레비전을 봐요.

I wear glasses.
안경을 써요.

↓

I have bad eyesight.
눈이 _____.

↓

I have to wear glasses.
안경을 _____.

↓

I have really bad eyesight.
눈이 ____ 안 좋아요.

If I want to watch TV, I have to wear glasses.
텔레비전을 _____ 안경을 써야 해요.

↓

I have really bad eyesight, so I have to wear glasses if I want to watch TV.
눈이 너무 안 _____ 텔레비전을 보려면 안경을 써야 해요.

💬 눈 좋아요?
= Do you have good eyesight?

아니요. ⎯⎯⎯⎯⎯⎯⎯⎯⎯⎯⎯
= No. I have bad eyesight.

💬 많이요?
= Very bad?

네. ⎯⎯⎯⎯⎯⎯⎯⎯⎯⎯⎯
= Yes. I have really bad eyesight.

💬 그럼 이거 안 보여요?
= Then you cannot see this?

네. ⎯⎯⎯⎯⎯⎯⎯⎯⎯⎯⎯
= No. I have to wear glasses.

💬 텔레비전 볼 때도요?
= When you watch TV as well?

네. ⎯⎯⎯⎯⎯⎯⎯⎯⎯⎯⎯
⎯⎯⎯⎯⎯⎯⎯⎯⎯⎯⎯
= Yes. I have really bad eyesight, so I have to wear glasses
   if I want to watch TV.

ANSWERS: Speaking Practice

💬 눈 좋아요?
= Do you have good eyesight?

> 💬 아니요. 눈이 안 좋아요.
> = No. I have bad eyesight.

💬 많이요?
= Very bad?

> 💬 네. 눈이 너무 안 좋아요.
> = Yes. I have really bad eyesight.

💬 그럼 이거 안 보여요?
= Then you cannot see this?

> 💬 네. 안경을 써야 해요.
> = No. I have to wear glasses.

💬 텔레비전 볼 때도요?
= When you watch TV as well?

> 💬 네. 눈이 너무 안 좋아서 텔레비전을 보려면 안경을 써야 해요.
> = Yes. I have really bad eyesight, so I have to wear glasses if I want to watch TV.

24 /

젖은 옷을 안 갈아입고 밖에 나갔더니
감기에 걸린 것 같아요.

옷
clothes

갈아입다
to change

Present	I change (clothes). =
Past	I changed (clothes). =
Future	I will change (clothes). =

❯ I change my clothes. =

❯ I changed my clothes. =

❯ I will change my clothes. =

나가다
to go out

Present	I go out. =
Past	I went out. =
Future	I will go out. =

감기
cold

걸리다
to catch

Present	I catch (a cold). =
Past	I caught (a cold). =
Future	I will catch (a cold). =

❯ I catch a cold. =

❯ I caught a cold. =

❯ I will catch a cold. =

ANSWERS: Conjugation Practice

옷

갈아입다

Present   I change (clothes). = 갈아입어요.

Past   I changed (clothes). = 갈아입었어요.

Future   I will change (clothes). = 갈아입을 거예요.

❯ I change my clothes. = 옷을 갈아입어요.

❯ I changed my clothes. = 옷을 갈아입었어요.

❯ I will change my clothes. = 옷을 갈아입을 거예요.

나가다

Present   I go out. = 나가요.

Past   I went out. = 나갔어요.

Future   I will go out. = 나갈 거예요.

감기

걸리다

Present   I catch (a cold). = 걸려요.

Past   I caught (a cold). = 걸렸어요.

Future   I will catch (a cold). = 걸릴 거예요.

❯ I catch a cold. = 감기에 걸려요.

❯ I caught a cold. = 감기에 걸렸어요.

❯ I will catch a cold. = 감기에 걸릴 거예요.

옷을 갈아입었어요.
I changed my clothes.

나갔어요.
I went out.

감기에 걸렸어요.
I caught a cold.

MODIFY
옷 with 젖다

ADD
밖에

젖은 옷을 갈아입었어요.
I changed out of my wet clothes.

CHANGE
the ending with
-(으)ㄴ 것 같다

CHANGE
the sentence to the
negative form using 안

밖에 나갔어요.
I went outside.

젖은 옷을 안 갈아입었어요.
I didn't change out of my wet clothes.

감기에 걸린 것 같아요.
I think I caught a cold.

COMBINE
two sentences by using -고

젖은 옷을 안 갈아입고 밖에 나갔어요.
I didn't change out of my wet clothes and went outside.

COMBINE
two sentences by using -더니

젖은 옷을 안 갈아입고 밖에 나갔더니 감기에 걸린 것 같아요.
I think I caught a cold because I didn't change out of my wet clothes and went outside.

I changed my clothes.
옷을 갈아입었어요.

I went out.
나갔어요.

I caught a cold.
감기에 걸렸어요.

I changed out of my wet clothes.
____ 옷을 갈아입었어요.

I went outside.
____ 나갔어요.

I didn't change out of my wet clothes.
젖은 옷을 __ 갈아입었어요.

I think I caught a cold.
감기에 _____.

I didn't change out of my wet clothes and went outside.
젖은 옷을 안 _____ 밖에 나갔어요.

I think I caught a cold because I didn't change out of my wet clothes and went outside.
젖은 옷을 안 갈아입고 밖에 _____ 감기에 걸린 것 같아요.

💬 감기 걸렸어요?
= You caught a cold?

네. ⬭⬭⬭⬭⬭⬭⬭⬭⬭⬭⬭⬭⬭
= Yes. I caught a cold.

💬 왜요?
= Why?

⬭⬭⬭⬭⬭⬭⬭⬭⬭⬭⬭⬭⬭
= I didn't change out of my wet clothes.

💬 왜요?
= Why?

귀찮아서 ⬭⬭⬭⬭⬭⬭⬭⬭⬭
⬭⬭⬭⬭⬭⬭⬭⬭
= It was such a bother, so I didn't change out of my wet clothes and went outside.

💬 그래서 감기에 걸렸어요?
= So you caught a cold?

네. ⬭⬭⬭⬭⬭⬭⬭⬭⬭⬭⬭⬭⬭
⬭⬭⬭⬭⬭⬭⬭⬭⬭⬭
= Yes. I think I caught a cold because I didn't change out of my wet clothes and went outside.

ANSWERS: Speaking Practice

💬 감기 걸렸어요?
= You caught a cold?

💬 네. 감기에 걸렸어요.
= Yes. I caught a cold.

💬 왜요?
= Why?

💬 젖은 옷을 안 갈아입었어요.
= I didn't change out of my wet clothes.

💬 왜요?
= Why?

💬 귀찮아서 젖은 옷을 안 갈아입고 밖에
나갔어요.
= It was such a bother, so I didn't change out of my wet
clothes and went outside.

💬 그래서 감기에 걸렸어요?
= So you caught a cold?

💬 네. 젖은 옷을 안 갈아입고 밖에 나갔더니
감기에 걸린 것 같아요.
= Yes. I think I caught a cold because I didn't change out
of my wet clothes and went outside.

25

아침에 빨리 준비하고 나가려면
머리는 저녁에 감고 자야 돼요.

준비하다
to get ready

Present   I get ready. =

Past   I got ready. =

Future   I will get ready. =

나가요
to go out

Present   I go out. =

Past   I went out. =

Future   I will go out. =

머리
hair

감다
to wash

Present   I wash (my hair). =

Past   I washed (my hair). =

Future   I will wash (my hair). =

❯ I wash my hair. =

❯ I washed my hair. =

❯ I will wash my hair. =

자다
to sleep

Present   I sleep. =

Past   I slept. =

Future   I will sleep. =

ANSWERS: Conjugation Practice

✎ **준비하다**

Present   I get ready. = 준비해요.

Past   I got ready. = 준비했어요.

Future   I will get ready. = 준비할 거예요.

✎ **나가요**

Present   I go out. = 나가요.

Past   I went out. = 나갔어요.

Future   I will go out. = 나갈 거예요.

✎ **머리**

✎ **감다**

Present   I wash (my hair). = 감아요.

Past   I washed (my hair). = 감았어요.

Future   I will wash (my hair). = 감을 거예요.

❯ I wash my hair. = 머리를 감아요.

❯ I washed my hair. = 머리를 감았어요.

❯ I will wash my hair. = 머리를 감을 거예요.

✎ **자다**

Present   I sleep. = 자요.

Past   I slept. = 잤어요.

Future   I will sleep. = 잘 거예요.

준비해요.
I get ready.

머리를 감아요.
I wash my hair.

자요.
I sleep.

ADD 아침에
↓

나가요.
I go out.

ADD 저녁에
↓

CHANGE
the ending with
-아/어/여야 되다
↓

아침에 준비해요.
I get ready in the morning.

머리를 저녁에 감아요.
I wash my hair in the evening.

자야 돼요.
I have to sleep.

ADD 빨리
↓

CHANGE
the object marker to the
topic marker -는
↓

아침에 빨리 준비해요.
I get ready quickly in the morning.

머리는 저녁에 감아요.
I wash at least my hair in the evening.

↓

COMBINE
two sentences by using -고
↓

↓

아침에 빨리 준비하고 나가요.
I get ready quickly and go out in the morning.

COMBINE
two sentences by using -고
↓

머리는 저녁에 감고 자야 돼요.
I have to wash at least my hair in the evening
before I sleep.

↓

COMBINE
two sentences by using -(으)려면
↓

아침에 빨리 준비하고 나가려면 머리는 저녁에 감고 자야 돼요.
If I want to get ready quickly before going out in the morning,
I have to wash at least my hair in the evening before I sleep.

REVIEW: Extension Practice

I get ready.
준비해요.

I wash my hair.
머리를 감아요.

자요.
I sleep.

나가요.
I go out.

↓

I get ready in the morning.
_____ 준비해요.

↓

I wash my hair in the evening.
머리를 _____ 감아요.

↓

↓

I have to sleep.
_____.

I get ready quickly in the morning.
아침에 ____ 준비해요.

↓

I wash at least my hair in the evening.
_____ 저녁에 감아요.

↓

I get ready quickly and go out in the morning.
아침에 빨리 _____ 나가요.

↓

I have to wash at least my hair in the evening before I sleep.
머리는 저녁에 ____ 자야 돼요.

↓

If I want to get ready quickly before going out in the morning,
I have to wash at least my hair in the evening before I sleep.
아침에 빨리 준비하고 _____ 머리는 저녁에 감고 자야 돼요.

💬 우리 내일 아침 일찍 나가야 돼요.
= We have to go out early tomorrow morning.

네.
= Okay. I get ready quickly in the morning.

💬 좋아요.
= Good.

대신
= Because I wash my hair in the evening instead.

💬 아, 아침에 안 감아요?
= Ah, you don't wash your hair in the morning?

네.
= No. I have to wash at least my hair in the evening before I sleep.

💬 그럼 머리 다 말리고 잘 거예요?
= So are you going to sleep after you dry your hair completely?

네.

= Yes. If I want to get ready quickly before going out in the morning,
   I have to wash at least my hair in the evening before I sleep.

ANSWERS: Speaking Practice

💬 우리 내일 아침 일찍 나가야 돼요.
= We have to go out early tomorrow morning.

💬 네. 저는 아침에 빨리 준비해요.
= Okay. I get ready quickly in the morning.

💬 좋아요.
= Good.

💬 대신 머리를 저녁에 감아요.
= Because I wash my hair in the evening instead.

💬 아, 아침에 안 감아요?
= Ah, you don't wash your hair in the morning?

💬 네. 머리는 저녁에 감고 자야 돼요.
= No. I have to wash at least my hair in the evening before I sleep.

💬 그럼 머리 다 말리고 잘 거예요?
= So are you going to sleep after you dry your hair completely?

💬 네. 아침에 빨리 준비하고 나가려면 머리는 저녁에 감고 자야 돼요.
= Yes. If I want to get ready quickly before going out in the morning, I have to wash at least my hair in the evening before I sleep.

26

몸에 비누칠하고 따뜻한 물을 틀었는데,
물이 차가워서 깜짝 놀랐어요.

비누칠하다
to lather up
with soap

Present   I lather it.   =

Past   I lathered it.   =

Future   I will lather it.   =

물
water

틀다
to turn on

Present   I turn on (something).   =

Past   I turned on (something).   =

Future   I will turn on (something).   =

❯ I turn on the water.   =

❯ I turned on the water.   =

❯ I will turn on the water.   =

물
water

차갑다
to be cold

Present   It is cold.   =

Past   It was cold.   =

Future   It will be cold.   =

❯ The water is cold.   =

❯ The water was cold.   =

❯ The water will be cold.   =

놀라다
to be surprised

Present   I am surprised.   =

Past   I was surprised.   =

Future   I will be surprised.   =

ANSWERS: Conjugation Practice

비누칠하다

Present   I lather it. = 비누칠해요.

Past   I lathered it. = 비누칠했어요.

Future   I will lather it. = 비누칠할 거예요.

물

Present   I turn on (something). = 틀어요.

Past   I turned on (something). = 틀었어요.

틀다

Future   I will turn on (something). = 틀 거예요.

❯ I turn on the water. = 물을 틀어요.

❯ I turned on the water. = 물을 틀었어요.

❯ I will turn on the water. = 물을 틀 거예요.

물

Present   It is cold. = 차가워요.

Past   It was cold. = 차가웠어요.

차갑다

Future   It will be cold. = 차가울 거예요.

❯ The water is cold. = 물이 차가워요.

❯ The water was cold. = 물이 차가웠어요.

❯ The water will be cold. = 물이 차가울 거예요.

놀라다

Present   I am surprised. = 놀라요.

Past   I was surprised. = 놀랐어요.

Future   I will be surprised. = 놀랄 거예요.

비누칠했어요.
I lathered (up something).

물을 틀었어요.
I turned on the water.

놀랐어요.
I was surprised.

ADD 몸에
↓

몸에 비누칠했어요.
I lathered up my body.

MODIFY
물 with 따뜻하다
↓

따뜻한 물을 틀었어요.
I turned on the warm water.

물이 차가웠어요.
The water was cold.

↓

COMBINE
two sentences by using -고
↓

ADD 깜짝
↓

깜짝 놀랐어요.
I was very surprised.

몸에 비누칠하고 따뜻한 물을 틀었어요.
I lathered up my body and turned on the warm water.

↓

COMBINE
two sentences by using -(으/느)ㄴ데
↓

몸에 비누칠하고 따뜻한 물을 틀었는데, 물이 차가웠어요.
I lathered up my body and turned on the warm water,
but the water was cold.

↓

COMBINE
two sentences by using -아/어/여서
↓

몸에 비누칠하고 따뜻한 물을 틀었는데, 물이 차가워서 깜짝 놀랐어요.
I lathered up my body and turned on the warm water, but the water was cold
so I was very surprised.

REVIEW: Extension Practice

I lathered (up something).
비누칠했어요.

I turned on the water.
물을 틀었어요.

I was surprised.
놀랐어요.

The water was cold.
물이 차가웠어요.

I lathered up my body.
____ 비누칠했어요.

I turned on the warm water.
_____ 물을 틀었어요.

I was very surprised.
____ 놀랐어요.

I lathered up my body and turned on the warm water.
몸에 _____ 따뜻한 물을 틀었어요.

I lathered up my body and turned on the warm water,
but the water was cold.
몸에 비누칠하고 따뜻한 물을 _____, 물이 차가웠어요.

I lathered up my body and turned on the warm water, but the water was cold
so I was very surprised.
몸에 비누칠하고 따뜻한 물을 틀었는데, 물이 _____ 깜짝 놀랐어요.

놀랐어요.

= I was surprised.

💬 왜요?

= Why?

= The water was cold.

💬 그래서 놀랐어요?

= That's why you were surprised?

네.

= Yes. I was very surprised.

💬 차가운 물을 틀었어요?

= Did you turn on the cold water?

아니요.

= No. I turned on the warm water, but the water was cold.

💬 그래서 놀랐어요?

= That's why you were surprised?

네.

= Yes. I lathered up my body and turned on the warm water, but the water was cold so I was very surprised.

ANSWERS: Speaking Practice

💬 놀랐어요.
= I was surprised.

💬 왜요?
= Why?

💬 물이 차가웠어요.
= The water was cold.

💬 그래서 놀랐어요?
= That's why you were surprised?

💬 네. 깜짝 놀랐어요.
= Yes. I was very surprised.

💬 차가운 물을 틀었어요?
= Did you turn on the cold water?

💬 아니요. 따뜻한 물을 틀었는데 물이 차가웠어요.
= No. I turned on the warm water, but the water was cold.

💬 그래서 놀랐어요?
= That's why you were surprised?

💬 네. 몸에 비누칠하고 따뜻한 물을 틀었는데, 물이 차가워서 깜짝 놀랐어요.
= Yes. I lathered up my body and turned on the warm water, but the water was cold so I was very surprised.

27 /

끼고 있는 렌즈 안 빼고 세수했어요?

렌즈
contact lenses

빼다
to take out

Present   I take out (something). =

Past   I took out (something). =

Future   I will take out (something). =

❯ I take out my contact lenses. =

❯ I took out my contact lenses. =

❯ I will take out my contact lenses. =

세수하다
to wash
one's face

Present   I wash my face. =

Past   I washed my face. =

Future   I will wash my face. =

ANSWERS: Conjugation Practice

렌즈

빼다

Present | I take out (something). = 빼요.

Past | I took out (something). = 뺐어요.

Future | I will take out (something). = 뺄 거예요.

❯ I take out my contact lenses. = 렌즈를 빼요.

❯ I took out my contact lenses. = 렌즈를 뺐어요.

❯ I will take out my contact lenses. = 렌즈를 뺄 거예요.

세수하다

Present | I wash my face. = 세수해요.

Past | I washed my face. = 세수했어요.

Future | I will wash my face. = 세수할 거예요.

렌즈 뺐어요.
I took out my contact lenses.

세수했어요.
I washed my face.

CHANGE
the sentence into a question.

↓

렌즈 뺐어요?
Did you take out your contact lenses?

CHANGE
the sentence into a question.

MODIFY
렌즈 with 끼고 있다

↓

끼고 있는 렌즈 뺐어요?
Did you take out the contact lenses
you were wearing?

↓

세수했어요?
Did you wash your face?

CHANGE
the sentence to the negative form using 안

↓

끼고 있는 렌즈 안 뺐어요?
Did you not take out the contact lenses
you were wearing?

↓

COMBINE
two sentences by using -고

↓

끼고 있는 렌즈 안 빼고 세수했어요?
Did you wash your face without taking out the contact lenses you were wearing?

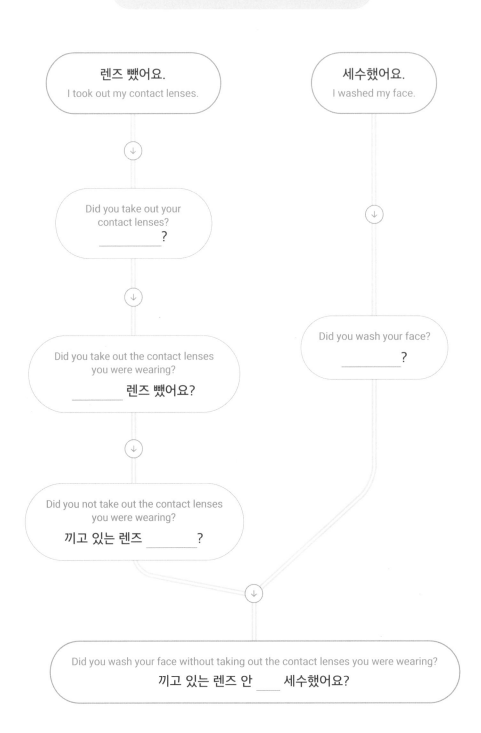

렌즈 뺐어요.
I took out my contact lenses.

세수했어요.
I washed my face.

Did you take out your contact lenses?
_____?

Did you take out the contact lenses you were wearing?
_____ 렌즈 뺐어요?

Did you wash your face?
_____?

Did you not take out the contact lenses you were wearing?
끼고 있는 렌즈 _____?

Did you wash your face without taking out the contact lenses you were wearing?
끼고 있는 렌즈 안 ____ 세수했어요?

= Did you wash your face?

💬 네.
= Yes.

= Did you take out the contact lenses you were wearing?

💬 아니요.
= No.

= Did you not take out the contact lenses you were wearing?

💬 네. 안 뺐어요.
= No, I didn't.

= Did you wash your face without taking out the contact lenses you were wearing?

💬 네.
= Yes.

ANSWERS: Speaking Practice

💬 세수했어요?
= Did you wash your face?

💬 네.
= Yes.

💬 끼고 있는 렌즈 뺐어요?
= Did you take out the contact lenses you were wearing?

💬 아니요.
= No.

💬 끼고 있는 렌즈 안 뺐어요?
= Did you not take out the contact lenses you were wearing?

💬 네. 안 뺐어요.
= No, I didn't.

💬 끼고 있는 렌즈 안 빼고 세수했어요?
= Did you wash your face without taking out the contact lenses you were wearing?

💬 네.
= Yes.

28 /

세수하고 깨끗한 수건으로 얼굴을
닦은 다음에 로션을 발랐어요?

세수하다
to wash
one's face

Present   I wash my face.   =

Past   I washed my face.   =

Future   I will wash my face.   =

얼굴
face

닦다
to wipe

Present   I wipe.   =

Past   I wiped.   =

Future   I will wipe.   =

❯ I wipe my face.   =

❯ I wiped my face.   =

❯ I will wipe my face.   =

로션
lotion

바르다
to apply

Present   I apply it.   =

Past   I applied it.   =

Future   I will apply it.   =

❯ I apply lotion.   =

❯ I applied lotion.   =

❯ I will apply lotion.   =

TRACK 82   **ANSWERS: Conjugation Practice**

세수하다
Present | I wash my face. = 세수해요.
Past | I washed my face. = 세수했어요.
Future | I will wash my face. = 세수할 거예요.

얼굴

닦다
Present | I wipe. = 닦아요.
Past | I wiped. = 닦았어요.
Future | I will wipe. = 닦을 거예요.

❯ I wipe my face. = 얼굴을 닦아요.
❯ I wiped my face. = 얼굴을 닦았어요.
❯ I will wipe my face. = 얼굴을 닦을 거예요.

로션

바르다
Present | I apply it. = 발라요.
Past | I applied it. = 발랐어요.
Future | I will apply it. = 바를 거예요.

❯ I apply lotion. = 로션을 발라요.
❯ I applied lotion. = 로션을 발랐어요.
❯ I will apply lotion. = 로션을 바를 거예요.

세수했어요.
I washed my face.

얼굴을 닦았어요.
I wiped my face.

로션을 발랐어요.
I applied lotion.

CHANGE
the sentence into a question.

CHANGE
the sentence into a question.

CHANGE
the sentence into a question.

얼굴을 닦았어요?
Did you wipe your face?

세수했어요?
Did you wash your face?

로션을 발랐어요?
Did you apply lotion?

ADD 수건으로

수건으로 얼굴을 닦았어요?
Did you wipe your face with a towel?

MODIFY 수건 with 깨끗하다

깨끗한 수건으로 얼굴을 닦았어요?
Did you wipe your face with a clean towel?

COMBINE
two sentences by using -고

세수하고 깨끗한 수건으로 얼굴을 닦았어요?
Did you wash your face and wipe it with a clean towel?

COMBINE
two sentences by using -(으)ㄴ 다음에

세수하고 깨끗한 수건으로 얼굴을 닦은 다음에 로션을 발랐어요?
Did you apply lotion after washing your face and wiping it with a clean towel?

251

REVIEW: Extension Practice

I washed my face.
세수했어요.

I wiped my face.
얼굴을 닦았어요.

I applied lotion.
로션을 발랐어요.

↓

Did you wipe your face?
_____?

↓

Did you wash your face?
_____?

Did you apply lotion?
_____?

↓

Did you wipe your face with a towel?
_____ 얼굴을 닦았어요?

↓

Did you wipe your face with a clean towel?
_____ 수건으로 얼굴을 닦았어요?

↓

Did you wash your face and wipe it with a clean towel?
_____ 깨끗한 수건으로 얼굴을 닦았어요?

↓

Did you apply lotion after washing your face and wiping it with a clean towel?
세수하고 깨끗한 수건으로 얼굴을 _____ 로션을 발랐어요?

[blank]

= Did you wash your face?

💬 네.
= Yes.

[blank]

= Did you wash and wipe your face?

💬 네. 닦았어요.
= Yes. I wiped it.

[blank]

= Did you wash your face and wipe it with a clean towel?

💬 네.
= Yes.

[blank]

[blank]

= Did you apply lotion after washing your face
and wiping it with a clean towel?

💬 네. 발랐어요.
= Yes. I applied some.

ANSWERS: Speaking Practice

💬 세수했어요?
   = Did you wash your face?

💬 네.
   = Yes.

💬 세수하고 얼굴을 닦았어요?
   = Did you wash and wipe your face?

💬 네. 닦았어요.
   = Yes. I wiped it.

💬 세수하고 깨끗한 수건으로 얼굴을 닦았어요?
   = Did you wash your face and wipe it with a clean towel?

💬 네.
   = Yes.

💬 세수하고 깨끗한 수건으로 얼굴을 닦은 다음에
로션을 발랐어요?
   = Did you apply lotion after washing your face and wiping it with
   a clean towel?

💬 네. 발랐어요.
   = Yes. I applied some.

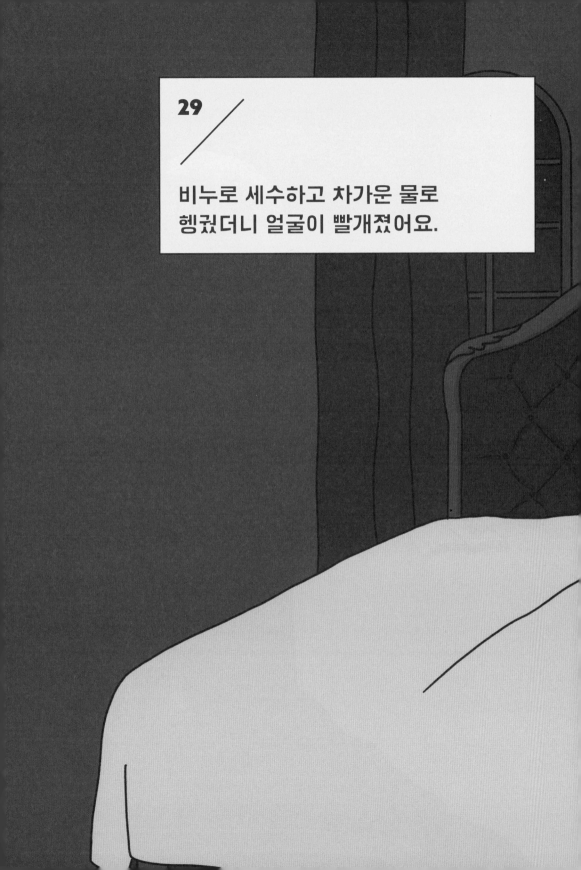

29

비누로 세수하고 차가운 물로
헹궜더니 얼굴이 빨개졌어요.

세수하다
to wash
one's face

Present   I wash my face.   =

Past   I washed my face.   =

Future   I will wash my face.   =

물
water

헹구다
to rinse

Present   I rinse.   =

Past   I rinsed.   =

Future   I will rinse.   =

❯ I rinse with water.   =

❯ I rinsed with water.   =

❯ I will rinse with water.   =

얼굴
face

빨갛다
to be red

Present   It is red.   =

Past   It was red.   =

Future   It will be red.   =

❯ One's face is red.   =

❯ One's face was red.   =

❯ One's face will be red.   =

TRACK 85

세수하다

Present | I wash my face. = 세수해요.

Past | I washed my face. = 세수했어요.

Future | I will wash my face. = 세수할 거예요.

물

Present | I rinse. = 헹궈요.

헹구다

Past | I rinsed. = 헹궜어요.

Future | I will rinse. = 헹굴 거예요.

> I rinse with water. = 물로 헹궈요.

> I rinsed with water. = 물로 헹궜어요.

> I will rinse with water. = 물로 헹굴 거예요.

얼굴

Present | It is red. = 빨개요.

빨갛다

Past | It was red. = 빨갰어요.

Future | It will be red. = 빨갈 거예요.

> One's face is red. = 얼굴이 빨개요.

> One's face was red. = 얼굴이 빨갰어요.

> One's face will be red. = 얼굴이 빨갈 거예요.

세수했어요.
I washed my face.

물로 헹궜어요.
I rinsed with water.

얼굴이 빨갰어요.
My face was red.

ADD
비누로

MODIFY
물 with 차갑다

CHANGE
the ending with
-아/어/여지다

↓

비누로 세수했어요.
I washed my face with soap.

↓

차가운 물로 헹궜어요.
I rinsed with cold water.

↓

COMBINE
two sentences by using -고

↓

얼굴이 빨개졌어요.
My face has turned red.

↓

비누로 세수하고 차가운 물로 헹궜어요.
I washed my face with soap and rinsed with cold water.

↓

COMBINE
two sentences by using -더니

↓

비누로 세수하고 차가운 물로 헹궜더니 얼굴이 빨개졌어요.
I washed my face with soap and rinsed with cold water, and now it has turned red.

I washed my face.
세수했어요.

I rinsed with water.
물로 헹궜어요.

My face was red.
얼굴이 빨갰어요.

↓

I washed my face with soap.
_____ 세수했어요.

↓

I rinsed with cold water.
_____ 물로 헹궜어요.

↓

My face has turned red.
얼굴이 _____.

↓

I washed my face with soap and rinsed with cold water.
비누로 _____ 차가운 물로 헹궜어요.

↓

I washed my face with soap and rinsed with cold water, and now it has turned red.
비누로 세수하고 차가운 물로 _____ 얼굴이 빨개졌어요.

💬 얼굴이 빨개요.
   = Your face is red.

        ┌─────────────────────────────┐
        └─────────────────────────────┘
        = I washed my face.

💬 어떻게요?
   = How?

        ┌─────────────────────────────────────┐
        └─────────────────────────────────────┘
        = I washed my face with soap and rinsed with water.

💬 뜨거운 물로요?
   = With hot water?

        아니요. ┌──────────────────────────────┐
              └──────────────────────────────┘
        = No. I washed my face with soap and rinsed with cold water.

💬 그래서 빨개졌어요?
   = That's why your face turned red?

        네. ┌─────────────────────────────────────┐
           └─────────────────────────────────────┘
        ┌─────────────────────────────┐
        └─────────────────────────────┘
        = Yes. I washed my face with soap and rinsed with cold water,
          and now it has turned red.

ANSWERS: Speaking Practice

💬 얼굴이 빨개요.
= Your face is red.

💬 세수했어요.
= I washed my face.

💬 어떻게요?
= How?

💬 비누로 세수하고 물로 헹궜어요.
= I washed my face with soap and rinsed with water.

💬 뜨거운 물로요?
= With hot water?

💬 아니요. 비누로 세수하고 차가운 물로 헹궜어요.
= No. I washed my face with soap and rinsed with cold water.

💬 그래서 빨개졌어요?
= That's why your face turned red?

💬 네. 비누로 세수하고 차가운 물로 헹궜더니
얼굴이 빨개졌어요.
= Yes. I washed my face with soap and rinsed with cold water,
and now it has turned red.

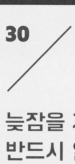

30

늦잠을 자지 않으려면 자기 전에
반드시 알람을 맞춰야 돼요.

늦잠을 자다
to oversleep,
to sleep in

Present   I oversleep. =

Past   I overslept. =

Future   I will oversleep. =

자다
to sleep

Present   I sleep. =

Past   I slept. =

Future   I will sleep. =

알람
alarm

맞추다
to set

Present   I set (an alarm). =

Past   I set (an alarm). =

Future   I will set (an alarm). =

❯ I set an alarm. =

❯ I set an alarm. =

❯ I will set an alarm. =

ANSWERS: Conjugation Practice

늦잠을
자다

Present   I oversleep. = 늦잠을 자요.

Past   I overslept. = 늦잠을 잤어요.

Future   I will oversleep. = 늦잠을 잘 거예요.

자다

Present   I sleep. = 자요.

Past   I slept. = 잤어요.

Future   I will sleep. = 잘 거예요.

알람

맞추다

Present   I set (an alarm). = 맞춰요.

Past   I set (an alarm). = 맞췄어요.

Future   I will set (an alarm). = 맞출 거예요.

❯ I set an alarm. = 알람을 맞춰요.

❯ I set an alarm. = 알람을 맞췄어요.

❯ I will set an alarm. = 알람을 맞출 거예요.

늦잠을 자요.
I oversleep.

자요.
I sleep.

알람을 맞춰요.
I set an alarm.

CHANGE
the ending with -**아/어/여야 되다**

↓

알람을 맞춰야 돼요.
I have to set an alarm.

ADD 반드시

↓

반드시 알람을 맞춰야 돼요.
I have to set an alarm no matter what.

CHANGE
the sentence to the negative form
using -**지 않다**

↓

늦잠을 자지 않아요.
I don't oversleep.

COMBINE
two sentences by using -**기 전에**

↓

자기 전에 반드시 알람을 맞춰야 돼요.
Before I sleep, I have to set an alarm no matter what.

COMBINE
two sentences by using -**(으)려면**

↓

늦잠을 자지 않으려면 자기 전에 반드시 알람을 맞춰야 돼요.
If I don't want to oversleep, I have to set an alarm no matter what before I sleep.

I oversleep.
늦잠을 자요.

I sleep.
자요.

I set an alarm.
알람을 맞춰요.

↓

I have to set an alarm.
알람을 _____.

↓

I have to set an alarm no matter what.
_____ 알람을 맞춰야 돼요.

↓

I don't oversleep.
늦잠을 _____.

Before I sleep, I have to set an alarm
no matter what.
_____ 반드시 알람을 맞춰야 돼요.

↓

If I don't want to oversleep, I have to set an alarm no matter what before I sleep.
늦잠을 자지 _____ 자기 전에 반드시 알람을 맞춰야 돼요.

💬 자주 늦잠 자요?
= Do you often oversleep?

아니요.
= No. I don't oversleep.

💬 아침에 잘 일어나요?
= Do you wake up easily in the morning?

아니요.
= No. I set an alarm.

💬 매일이요?
= Every day?

네.
= Yes. I have to set an alarm no matter what.

💬 안 그러면 늦잠 자요?
= Otherwise you oversleep?

네.

= Yes. If I don't want to oversleep, I have to set an alarm no matter what before I sleep.

ANSWERS: Speaking Practice

💬 자주 늦잠 자요?
= Do you often oversleep?

💬 아니요. 늦잠을 자지 않아요.
= No. I don't oversleep.

💬 아침에 잘 일어나요?
= Do you wake up easily in the morning?

💬 아니요. 알람을 맞춰요.
= No. I set an alarm.

💬 매일이요?
= Every day?

💬 네. 반드시 알람을 맞춰야 돼요.
= Yes. I have to set an alarm no matter what.

💬 안 그러면 늦잠 자요?
= Otherwise you oversleep?

💬 네. 늦잠을 자지 않으려면 자기 전에 반드시 알람을 맞춰야 돼요.
= Yes. If I don't want to oversleep, I have to set an alarm no matter what before I sleep.

/ Glossary

-(ㄴ/는)다	ending used to show your reaction or impression when talking about a present action or situation
-(으)ㄴ 다음에	after + V-ing
-(으)ㄹ게요	will
-(으)ㄹ까요?	Do you think it will...?
-(으)러 가다	to go (somewhere) in order to + V, to go for + V-ing/N
-(으)세요	imperative ending (polite)
-아/어/여 보이다	to look + adjective
5시	5 o'clock
가다	to go
가볍다	to be light
가져가다	to take or bring (something)
갈아입다	to change (clothes)
감기	a cold
감다	to wash (one's hair)
갑자기	suddenly
같이	together, with
(감기에) 걸리다	to catch (a cold)
검사	test
것 같다	I think...

겉	the outside
-겠-	suffix for showing intention or assumption
고맙다	to be grateful, to be thankful
고치다	to fix (something)
곧	soon
괜찮다	to be okay
귀찮다	to be a hassle, to be annoying
그것	that
그냥	just
그다음	after that, and then
그래서	so, that's why
그래요	exclamatory word used when reacting to someone with surprise or agreement
그러다	to do that, to act like that, to behave like that
그런데	but
그럼	then
그렇게	like that, that much
그리고	and
근데	but
급하다	to be urgent, to be hasty * 급하게 is the adverb form of 급하다.

기분	feelings	당황하다	to panic, to be flustered
깜짝	adverb used to describe how one is surprised	대신	instead
깨끗하다	to be clean	대충	roughly, cursorily
(렌즈를) 끼다	to wear (contact lenses)	더	more
나가다	to go out	더럽다	to be dirty
나다	to come out, to be made, to grow	덥다	to be hot
나쁘다	to be bad	덮다	to cover
나오다	to come out	-도	too, also
내일	tomorrow	되다¹	to become
너무	too, so, really	되다²	to be done, to be possible, to work
넘어지다	to fall over	두껍다	to be thick
네	yes	들다	to pick up (something)
놀라다	to be surprised	따뜻하다	to be warm
누구	who, whose	땀	sweat
눈	eye(s), eyesight	때	during, while, when
눕다	to lie (somewhere)	때문에	because (of), since
늦다	to be late	또	again
늦잠	sleeping late into the morning, getting up late	뜨겁다	to be hot
늦잠을 자다	to oversleep, to sleep in	렌즈	contact lenses
다	all, completely	로션	lotion
다래끼	stye	마스카라	mascara
다시	again	마시다	to drink
다치다	to get hurt	만나다	to meet
닦다	to wipe, to polish	많이	a lot
		말리다	to dry

맞다	to be right		별로	not really
맞추다[1]	to make something fit, to have something tailor-made		병원	hospital
			보다	to watch, to look
맞추다[2]	to set, to adjust		보이다	to be seen, can see (something)
매일	every day		-부터	from, since
머리	hair		비누	soap
면도하다	to shave		비누칠하다	to lather (something) with soap
모르다	to not know			
몸	body		비싸다	to be expensive
묶다	to tie		빌려주다	to lend
물	water		빗	comb
물놀이하다	to play in the water		빗다	to comb (one's hair)
뭐	what		빠지다	to fall out
뭘	what * 뭘 is short for 무엇을.		빨갛다	to be red
			빨리	quickly, fast
바로	right away		빼다	to take out (something)
바르다	to apply (something)		사다	to buy
바쁘다	to be busy		상처	cut, wound
밖	outside		새로	newly
반드시	at any cost		새벽	dawn, the time between 1 a.m. and sunrise
받다	to receive, to accept, to take, to get			
			생기다	to come into being, to be formed, to be created, to appear
밝다	to be bright			
번지다	to be smudged			
벌써	already		샴푸	shampoo
벗다	to take off		서다	to stand up
			세수하다	to wash (one's face)

수건	towel	어디	where
수염	beard, stubble	어떤	what kind of, which
시간	time	어떻게	how, what
시끄럽다	to be loud	어색하다	to feel awkward
시력	(eye)sight	어울리다	to look good on (someone), to suit someone
시력 검사	eyesight test		
시원하다	to be cool, to be refreshing	어제	yesterday
		언제	when
신다	to put on, to wear (shoes)	얼굴	face
		얼른	quickly
쓰다[1]	to use	없다	to be not have, to not exist, to be not there
쓰다[2]	to put on, to wear (glasses)		
아	oh, ah	예쁘다	to be pretty
아니요	no	오래되다	to be old
아침	morning	오랜만에	after a long time, first time in a long while
안	not		
안 그러면	otherwise	옷	clothes
안경	glasses	왜	why
안과	ophthalmology clinic	우리	we, our
알람	alarm	우와	wow
앞	front	운동하다	to exercise
약	medicine	(알람이) 울리다	to go off, to ring
약속	appointment, plan		
양말	socks	이	teeth
양치하다	to brush one's teeth	이거	this, this one
어둡다	to be dark	이불	blanket, bedding
		이제	now, now that

일어나다	to get up, to wake up	준비하다	to get ready
일찍	early	지워지다	to come off, to be erased
입다	to put on, to wear	진짜	really, real
있다	to be there, to have, to exist	(화장이) 진하다	to be heavy, to be thick
자다	to sleep	집	house, home
자라다	to grow	짜다	to squeeze
자주	often	짧다	to be short
작다	to be small	차갑다	to be cold, to be chilly
-잖아요	ending commonly used when you say something the listener already knows or should know, or when you are correcting what someone says	챙기다	to take, to pack
		춥다	to be cold
		(커튼을) 치다	to draw, to close (curtains)
잘	well	치료	treatment
저	I, me (honorific)	치약	toothpaste
저녁	evening	친구	friend
전부	all, entirely	침대	bed
정말	really, very	칫솔	toothbrush
젖다	to get wet	커튼	curtain
제	my (honorific) * 제 is short for 저의.	커피	coffee
		컵	cup
조금	a little	크다	to be big
졸리다	to be sleepy	텔레비전	television
좀	a little, please	틀다	to turn on
좋다	to be good, to be likable, to be desirable, to be nice, to like	피곤하다	to be tired
		필요하다	to need
		하다	to do

학교	school
한 번	one time
항상	always
헤어드라이어	hairdryer
헹구다	to rinse
화장	makeup
화장품	cosmetics
화장하다	to put on makeup, to wear makeup
회사	company, office
효과	effect
(땀을) **흘리다**	to sweat

점점 길어지는 한국어 문장